THE IRISH CENTURY

THE IRISH CENTURY

Michael MacCarthy Morrogh

Foreword by Neil Jordan

Picture research by Bill Bagnell
and Mick Farrelly

ROBERTS RINEHART PUBLISHERS

Boulder, Colorado

Half title: Belfast children playing in the street, 1913. Title spread: Haymaking at the turn of the century, the Clogher valley, County Fermanagh. Above: Church of Ireland Bishop Lewis Crosby and wife, at an exhibition of modern painting in Dublin, circa 1950. Opposite: Children try to catch bubbles blown by a villager.

Published by
ROBERTS RINEHART PUBLISHERS
6309 Monarch Park Place
Niwot, Colorado 80503
Tel 303.652.2685
Fax 303.652.2689
www.robertsrinehart.com

Distributed to the trade by Publishers Group West

International Standard Book Number 1-57098-237-6

Library of Congress Catalog Card Number 98-85562

Published in the UK and Ireland by
Weidenfeld & Nicolson

Printed by Nuovo Istituto Italiano d'Arti Grafiche SpA, Bergamo, Italy

10 9 8 7 6 5 4 3 2 1

CONTENTS

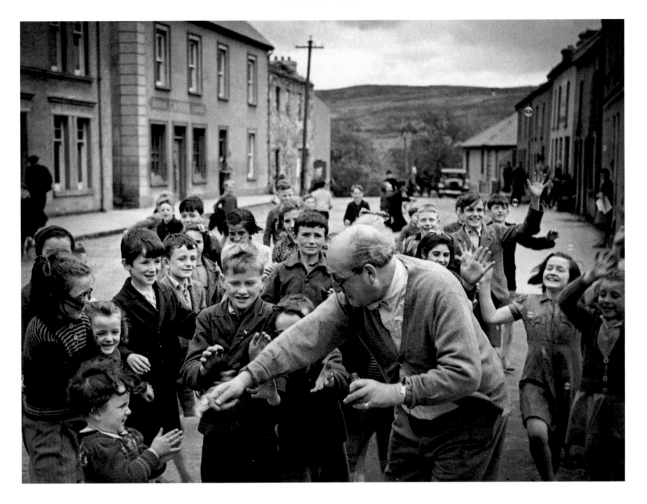

FOREWORD

The year 1998 could well be the first in Irish history when the past will be what it claims to be. It won't erupt into the present, providing a cloak under which the Irish can hide, or even a scarf with which to strangle themselves. In the Gaelic lessons at school – I was a beneficiary of the Republic's education system – there was a tense called the 'gnáthchaite'. 'Gnáth' means continuous and 'chaite' means past: continuous past. Though I'm no grammatical expert, I don't think there is an equivalent in English grammar.

The concept of a continuous past would seem to be an absurdity. But this is the tense that we Irish have been condemned to live in, the tense we might now be emerging from.

Like the unquiet ghost in *Hamlet* or the restless dead of horror movies, the past that impinges unnaturally on the present gives rise to monsters. This book opens with a picture of an eviction and with Gladstone's attempt to push through the Home Rule Bill in 1886; it concludes with the recent peace talks. It admirably documents and pictures the years in between, in the course of which those monsters were many times thought to have exhausted themselves. The fact that they hadn't says more about the importance of history, memory and language to the body politic than I would like to imagine. The gnáthchaite continued his business, haunting and intermittently causing eruptions of violence. And one can only hope, now that his rule is over, that the gnáthchaite will be confined within the body of a beautiful language, like the coccyx or the appendix, an important reminder of a function that once was.

NEIL JORDAN
May 1998

Opposite: Workers at the
Guinness Brewery, Dublin, photographed by Bert Hardy.
Overleaf: A round tower appears above the woods at
Glendalough, County Wicklow.

EDITOR'S NOTE

The inspiration for this book was the extensive collection of photojournalism at the Hulton Getty Collection which is especially good on the political history of Ireland. Other photographs reproduced in this book have been researched from public and private archives in the United Kingdom and the Republic of Ireland. Additional key sources include the remarkable images recorded by Father Browne who captured Irish domestic and political life with perceptive insight from 1920 to about 1940. The Cashman Collection within the RTE archives is also excellent on the Civil War period. Sean Sexton's images of late 19th- and early 20th-century life are remarkable. Dublin society photographer George Duncan has left behind a wonderful record of Ireland from the 1940s through to the 1970s. Klaus Francke's dramatic images are often especially good on Irish folk and ways. Finally, the portraiture of Bobby Hanvey earned the confidence of people from all sections of the Northern Irish community.

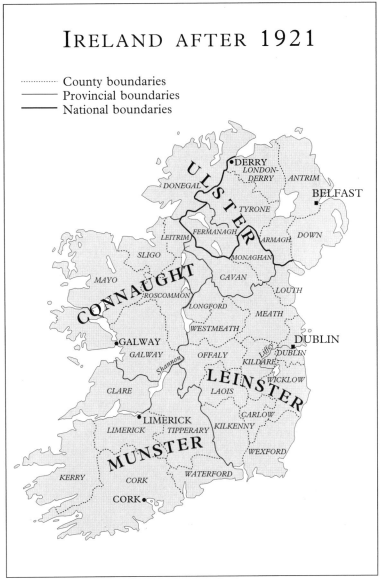

IRELAND AFTER 1921

············ County boundaries
———— Provincial boundaries
━━━━ National boundaries

PROLOGUE

A cottage under siege. *A battering ram in action at an eviction on the Vandeleur Estate during the height of the struggle between landlords and tenants in the late 1880s. Dubbed the Plan of Campaign by the nationalist Land League, this was a concerted attempt by tenants to obtain rent reductions in response to the agricultural depression of those years. Some landlords knuckled under, but others demanded their rents, and were prepared to evict their tenants if they did not get them. Battering rams were rarely used since they destroyed the property, but some tenants barricaded themselves in, creating 'standing fortifications. Huge trunks of timber and immense ledges of limestone have been removed into many houses.' The Land League seized upon such moments for their propaganda value, and from the relaxed posture of the onlookers this might be a staged photograph, even though taken during the course of a real eviction.*

O F ALL THE GREAT OCCASIONS IN THE HOUSE of Commons during the 19th century few were so full of tension and excitement as the introduction and subsequent defeat of Mr Gladstone's first Home Rule Bill. The first reading took place at 4.30 pm on 8 April 1886. 'The scene in the lobby was a lively one,' wrote an observer. The Princess of Wales was seated in the ladies' cage – the old grill-covered ladies' gallery where it was said that a patch of brass railing had been polished bright over the years by Mrs Gladstone, while witnessing gargantuan parliamentary performances by her husband. In turn the despatch boxes were supposed to bear the marks of Mr Gladstone's furiously pounding knuckles.

The floor of the House was packed, with extra chairs arranged in double rows. MPs had been booking their seats since the early hours of the morning by leaving hats on the benches. According to the *Punch* diarist (surprisingly neutral in his sympathies), once breakfast time approached and the House emptied, one playful member switched the hats. 'Great row when Parnellites came back. Decided that it must be the Ulster members who had done it. Major Saunderson [the Ulster leader] entering, quarter of an hour later, received with yell of execration.'

In the late afternoon, dressed in his traditional high collar (a gift to cartoonists) and, unusually, a rose in his buttonhole, Mr Gladstone entered the chamber. The ruling Liberal party and their allies, the Irish party, leapt to their feet, cheering and waving their hats – a more stylish gesture than the present feeble flapping of order papers. The Tory opposition naturally sat in their seats; but ominously so did a group at the back of the government benches. Leading this recalcitrant squad, and looking very uncomfortable cheek by jowl, were the two leaders of these anti-Home Rule Liberals, Lord Hartington, heir to the Duke of Devonshire, representing the conservative Whiggish faction, and Joseph Chamberlain, 'Radical Joe', the scourge of the landed interest since his entry into Parliament in 1876.

Aided by his special mixture of raw egg and sherry, Gladstone spoke for three-and-a-half hours in what was generally regarded as the finest speech of his career, which had stretched to 63 years by his retirement in 1894. His message was that the time had come to embrace the driving aim of the main Irish party, summed up quite simply by its very name – Home Rule.

It involved creating a parliament in Dublin for the conduct of domestic Irish affairs; imperial affairs – in effect foreign policy and defence – would be controlled still by Westminster. Such a parliament would be rather more than a revival of the Irish Parliament which had sat in Dublin until the Act of

The Grand Old Man. *Mr Gladstone towards the end of his 63 years of active political service, which included being Prime Minister four times, the last when 84 years old. Here the GOM has removed his hat for the photographer, revealing the 'prodigious headpiece' which read 20,000 books, and poured forth an unceasing tide of words in speech and print as he sought to run the most powerful country in the world.*

Bound for far Amerikay. *One final indignity awaits emigrants at Queenstown (Cobh), near Cork, which had become the major port of embarkation: an eye inspection by the ship's doctor for glaucoma. Emigration proved to be the safety valve for Ireland's excess population with the numbers going down from 8 to 4¼ million in the years from the Great Famine of the 1840s until the 1960s. Emigrants tended to be young: 'The pick and flower of the land, so to speak, are going.'* [PHOTO: FR. BROWNE S. J.]

Union in 1800. It was not independence for Ireland, but neither was it merely an extension of local government. The key concession was a law-making body, a parliament, which would appoint and control the Irish executive.

The Irish wish for some form of self government, to be achieved constitutionally and peacefully, was not new. Once emancipation – the right for catholics to sit in parliament – had been won by the efforts of Daniel O'Connell in 1829, the great man turned his attention towards repeal of the Union. Parliament should return for Ireland; but no longer be exclusively protestant and therefore unrepresentative. O'Connell, however, had not realised that if the Act of Union was simply repealed, not only would the Dublin parliament return but also an English executive appointed and controlled from London. Isaac Butt spotted this omission and accordingly formed his Home Rule party in the early 1870s, rather than revamp O'Connell's repeal movement – which in any case had faded away in the 1840s.

Soon after Butt's death in 1879, the Irish Home Rule party was being led by the commanding figure of Charles Stewart Parnell, someone who could match the heroic status of O'Connell in the first half of the century. By the mid 1880s he had so disciplined his party to take advantage of the new elec-

toral franchise that they had gained a clear majority of 85 among the 103 seats allocated to Ireland. Apart from the 16 seats in north-east Ulster, and the two reserved for Dublin University (Trinity College), Parnell could put himself forward as representing Ireland. With the Prime Minister of Britain in alliance, it seemed as if nothing could stop the passage of the Home Rule Bill that summer of 1886.

But Gladstone, perhaps more than Parnell, reckoned without the unpopularity of the measure in England. To supporters of Home Rule, it was simply a matter of justice. Over four-fifths of Ireland had spoken. Ulster's position (it was assumed) was largely bluster; and in any case, was it right for the tail to wag the dog? Rejection of the bill would entail a return to coercion for Ireland – exceptional laws to deal with a justly frustrated people. For Gladstone Home Rule was the way to effect a final solution to the Irish problem – and to preserve the framework of the United Kingdom.

In public, Parnell would echo these sentiments; but earlier, in the fiery stage of his career, he had hinted that Home Rule might be a stepping stone to eventual separation. And certainly this was one of the reasons why the bill was opposed in England. It threatened both the unity of the Empire and of the United Kingdom. That dread object, which so alarms the politically timid, might have been unleashed – a precedent. Where would the process stop? Besides, went another argument, the Irish might be a majority in Ireland, but the correct unit to consider was the United Kingdom, where their numbers were in a minority and their attitude therefore traitorous. Ulster's feelings were inflamed by the rhetoric of Lord Randolph Churchill. Joseph Chamberlain was adept at pinpointing the practical difficulties of framing a satisfactory Home Rule bill, and in a series of brilliant speeches focused on the issue of Irish members continuing, or not, at Westminster once the Dublin parliament had been formed – the 'West Lothian question' of today. There was no answer to it then, just as there can be no answer now.

Perhaps the strongest objection, but rarely articulated, was the racial belief that the Irish were unworthy of representative

institutions. One of the Victorian images of Ireland had long been of a repellent land crawling with low-browed, strong-jawed, snub-nosed simian creatures, knuckles raw from brushing the ground, their ragged clothing concealing blunderbusses, pikes, and other articles of destruction. The picture had been toned down by the 1880s, when the country tended to be represented by the beautiful Pre-Raphaelite damsel, 'Hibernia', though still liable to dreadful assaults by nationalist ruffians. Yet the Marquis of Salisbury, leader of the Conservative party, was sufficiently patrician to be able to air his prejudices without fear of losing status. In a marvellously relaxed address he explained that there were races like the Hottentots and Hindoos – and Irish – incapable of self government. The recipe for that land was firm, imperial supervision, with the siphoning off of a million surplus Irishmen to the wastes of Manitoba in Canada.

At the heart of the frenzied debate in the Commons, over sixteen nights, as well as at a number of meetings outside, was the deep lack of sympathy the English have for nationalism. Never having had to fight for their independence for nearly a thousand years, they cannot understand the passions that one's nation can arouse. Embedded within the English objection was the puzzlement, grief and eventual anger that a body of adja-

cent people, however defined, should *choose* to throw off their allegiance to the superior country.

Commentators agree that the speeches in that last debate were of the highest quality ending with Gladstone, the unflagging veteran, on his feet for 'only' one hour and forty minutes, not bad for a man of 76. His final appeal was that the House 'think well, think wisely, think not for the moment, but for the years that are to come, before you reject this bill.' And reject the bill is what the House of Commons did, by 341 votes to 311.

Gladstone bounced back with a second Home Rule bill in 1893 and this time it passed the Commons, accompanied one night by fisticuffs involving forty MPs; but it then progressed to the House of Lords to be rejected by a contemptuous and overwhelming majority. It has been the fashion among historians for some time to judge Gladstone's efforts to pass Home Rule for Ireland as little more than electoral manoeuvrings – stratagems which failed, moreover, since it split his party and shackled it to a most unpopular policy. But the history of Ireland in the 20th century might seem to suggest that Mr Gladstone's attempts were indeed a lost chance. 'What fools we were', remarked King George V to Ramsey MacDonald in 1930, after Ireland's eventual independence, 'not to have accepted Gladstone's Home Rule Bill.'

CHAPTER ONE

THE
TWO IRELANDS

Good times. *Ireland had twenty years of quiet around the turn of the century, typified by this party thrown on the 'Bangor Boat' in County Down to celebrate the opening of a new bakery by the Co-operative Society in Belfast in 1906. Relations between workers and management were generally better in Ireland at this time than in England.*
[PHOTO: FRANCIS J. BIGGAR]

THE GREATEST NOVEL OF THE 20TH CENTURY, James Joyce's *Ulysses*, is located in Dublin in 1904. Joyce chose that date because it was the year he and Nora Barnacle left Ireland; but it also symbolised a time when nothing much was happening on the public front. Dublin and most of Ireland appeared to have renounced nationalist matters and went about their business little troubled by the vapourings of politicians. The first decade of Ireland in the 20th century does not seem to belie our image of that gentle, familiar Edwardian period, when the season is always summer; cornets and trombones play on the bandstand; the ladies wear white, gentlemen boaters, small girls pinafores; and in the distance steam trains puff along, while the occasional cloud of dust can be seen from a pioneering motor-car.

Ireland had not always looked so peaceful and picturesque. Its history has been a cauldron of dispute and dissension, stirred by repeated invasions, garnished with some astonishing cultural achievements. An offshore island of an offshore island, it has appeared somewhat remote to Continentals. Polybius thought it was shaped like an egg, which is not a bad stab, though a saucer might be more appropriate topographically: a low-lying centre, boggy and wet, surrounded by uplands. Commonly described as 'mild, moist and changeable', rain is the persistent, element of the climate, but less feared than in Britain, indeed almost welcomed: a endlessly drizzling day is described as 'soft', while in west Cork visitors are proudly shown Mount Gabriel and informed, 'If you can see the mountain it's going to rain; and if you can't then it's raining.' Warmed by the Gulf Stream (though apparently some hand has turned this off, or at least down, for the last twenty years) the dramatic western coastline enjoys temperate winters and lush vegetation. At least two-thirds of Ireland is fine agricultural land, the rest being peat bog, mountain and scrub, yet with surprisingly few trees, for the country is amongst the least forested in Europe.

Quite recently, the remains of a Roman fort have been discovered north of Dublin, but what settlement there was must have been very brief, as the Roman Empire never extended to Ireland, although Agricola contemplated an invasion in AD 81. Any invasion, in fact, went the other way, in the 4th and 5th centuries, with raids from Ireland into western England and Wales (enslaving the future St Patrick), while the northern Irish, called Scotii, established themselves in western Scotland – Kintyre is just 14 miles off the Irish coast. As Europe col-

Victorians on tour *in 1859 stop at Kilcrea Abbey. The gentry's servant and donkey wait through the archway. Built by Cormac MacCarthy, lord of Muskerry, in 1465 for the Franciscans, the MacCarthy of Blarney who smooth-talked his way past Queen Elizabeth I is buried here.*
[PHOTO: WILLIAM ENGLAND]

At a holy well *(below) in 1900 – still to be seen in rural Ireland, although frowned upon by the Church.*
[PHOTO: FRANCIS J. BIGGAR]

The High Cross of Muiredach *(right) in the ruins of Monasterboice monastery, County Louth, built in the 9th century at a time when Ireland's Christian culture was at full throttle. In the background is a round tower, one of the 65 peculiar to Ireland, built both to the glory of God and as a defence against Viking sea-raiders.*

lapsed into the Dark Ages, Ireland experienced its heyday as the beacon of western civilisation and Christianity. 'The island of saints and Scholars' developed a potent culture which thrived not only at home but abroad.

Monks and missionaries moved to Scotland, northern England, then to the Continent, founding monasteries on the way. St Brendan made spectacular sea voyages and, it was claimed later, even discovered America, though it seems more likely to have been Madeira. Home in Ireland other monks busied themselves creating intricately illuminated manuscripts, such as the Book of Kells.

It all proved far too tempting a target for avaricious Vikings. During the 9th and 10th centuries they went through their repertoire of pillage and sacking – Clonmacnoise monastery looted ten times, Kildare sixteen – but some did

stay to found small river settlements which later became Ireland's chief towns – Dublin, Cork, Waterford, Limerick. Irish Gaelic society was rural and not urban, its wealth dependent on nomadic pastoral farming. Lack of political unity, however, allowed the Anglo-Normans a relatively easy conquest when they invaded in the 12th century. Soon the Normans found themselves sucked into the Gaelic world, and a fresh conquest was deemed necessary in the 16th century. This time the newcomers from Elizabethan England brought a different religion with them, which served to distinguish ruler from ruled. Land confiscations, followed by laws transforming catholics into second-class citizens, completed the process by which Ireland came under the control of a protestant ascendancy obedient to England.

Ulster's fine linen *originated with locally grown flax, which was then placed in ponds to rot the unwanted parts of the plant. Weighed down by stones, the flax languished underwater until pulled up by men (here in County Antrim, 1910) to be dried (above). The smell of this process, known as retting, marked the late summer weeks in the north.*

Winnowing corn. *A white-bearded Methuselah in the Mourne mountains in 1905 allows the wind to separate the grain from the chaff in an almost biblical scene (right).* [PHOTOS, ABOVE AND RIGHT: W. A. GREEN]

The industrial revolution largely by-passed Ireland, but the population still rose until the potato famine of 1846–49, when about one million died and another million emigrated; in figures this meant eight million suddenly became six million. From then on numbers steadily declined for the next 100 years and more, making Ireland a demographic freak amongst European nations. After these terrible times in the mid-19th century, however, a visitor to Ireland would not have seen many radical differences from Britain or western Europe. There may have been a greater number of poorer farmers, it is true, but cities existed (those Viking settlements) and the familiar infrastructure of communications. Railways operated, even on Sundays in the God-fearing north, despite opposition claiming that 'souls are sent to the devil at sixpence apiece … and every shout of the railway steam whistle is answered by a shout in hell.' Just to make things difficult, Ireland had its own gauge, midway between Brunel's and Stephenson's, as well as several charming light railways, the most bizarre of which was the Listowel–Ballybunion monorail which necessitated balancing passengers in the carriage on either side of the single rail.

Lazy beds, *raised potato plots created out of soil dug from the trenches on either side, and often fertilised with seaweed, cling to hills and along clifftops. Long snaky lines of abandoned beds can be seen all over Ireland, testimony to the desperate search for more cultivable land. Here women are using long locally made spades in Antrim to 'set' (plant) potatoes in 1905. There is a pile of stones collected off the beds under the gnarled trees.*
[PHOTO: R. WELCH]

Market day *in a small town in County Galway. The large scales are for weighing sacks of potatoes.*

A hand loom *for weaving a length of tweed in a cottage room.*

Winter fuel. *Women compacting dung, straw stubble and byre sweepings into cakes for burning on the fire, County Kilkenny. The two men carefully observe them at this work, one perched on a jaunting car, its seats running fore-and-aft.*

Peat is stacked *after being cut. Much of lowland Ireland, in the midlands and west, was peat bog, used then (and now) as a major fuel since the woods were long gone and coal had to be imported.*

Stick out your hand there, Mike! *Traffic in St Stephen's Green, the smart square in Dublin, hardly bustles in this scene from 1910.*

From the long perspective, Ireland at the turn of the century was right in the middle of an unaccustomed twenty-year quiescence. The excitements of Parnellism and Gladstone's Home Rule bills were past; premature manifestations of a more direct nationalism were yet to come. Queen Victoria's visit at the turn of the century had passed off without any untoward incidents. This was despite misgivings by the Queen as to Irish loyalties: whenever booing was heard on the rare occasions when she attended public ceremonies after Albert's death, the miscreants were 'probably socialist and the worst Irish'. The year 1904 is in fact exactly the date when a betting man would have plumped on the eventual disappearance of the Irish Question, not because of any one dramatic demarch, but the cumulative result of years of stability and apparent resignation to the status quo. Moreover, there had been crucial reforms which seemed to have lanced the boil of furious nationalism. The Conservative and Unionist governments of Lord Salisbury had taken the line of rigid opposition to Home Rule and, if necessary, coercion to keep order; but on social and economic matters they were prepared to go far. 'Killing Home Rule by kindness' was the phrase in vogue.

The reforms included an important local government act of 1898 and various regional economic advances, the latter sometimes in the teeth of obscurantist farmers or scoffing commentators. The novelist George Moore brutally satirised Horace Plunkett, founder of the Co-operative Movement and in effect minister for Irish agriculture, by depicting him as Bouvard, one half of Flaubert's pair of preternaturally stupid and earnest clerks. Easily the most far reaching of reforms concerned landholding. All four provinces of Ireland – Leinster, Munster, Connaught and Ulster, with a combined population of four and a half million – were largely agricultural economies. To many in the 19th century, the Irish Question had really been the Land Question: solve the latter and the former vanishes. It

Timeless in Killarney, *on a promontory of Lough Leane, County Kerry, stands Ross Castle, built by O'Donoghue Ross, and in the late 16th century awarded to the Brownes, Elizabethan settlers and afterwards Earls of Kenmare. Fortified peel towers were common, particularly in the south-west. The Brownes added a wing to the old castle, but in the 18th century decamped to a new house nearby.*

Prosperous holidaymakers *outside their hotel. The Victorians and Edwardians who could afford it flocked to Ireland in the summer months, particularly to see the beauties of Connemara and Kerry on the west coast. The well-protected wicker chairs rather give the lie to the sunshades, as do the children's coats.*

Sod-built cabins *had become tourist items by the 1910s, when this photograph (above) was taken. The little girl, the cat, the items in the window, even the sunny weather seem provided by central casting. There were thousands of such hovels in pre-Famine Ireland, but emigration, relative affluence and the weather – note the props holding up this structure – ensured their disappearance.*
[PHOTO: W. A. GREEN]

Many small towns and villages *looked as unprepossessing as this dreary line of thatched, single-storey houses on the outskirts giving way to slated roofs towards the centre. There was small danger of traffic disturbing the little girls' game in the centre of the road.*
[PHOTO: A. HOGG]

Family life *clustered around the kitchen hearth. Often the fire was at floor level, with pots and kettles hanging over or into it. There does not appear to be any oven for baking. Old and young would entertain each other with songs and stories.*
[PHOTO: ROSE SHAW]

was strongly held if rarely expressed, that the bulk of the land in Ireland belonged to 'the people' and not their landlords – a race apart in religion, identity and residence. The great dispossessions of the 17th century were not forgotten but brooded upon. This feeling of alienation was compounded by the Famine of 1846–49 and the wretched situation of tenants throughout most of the 19th century, their holdings insecure and evictions, at times, a common occurrence. Matters reached crisis point in the grandly named Land War of 1879–1882.

The war was ended by Mr Gladstone's use of coercion and concession. The Land Act of 1881 gave tenants some control over their rent; coupled with the earlier 1870 act they now enjoyed far greater security on the land. But why stop there? That folk memory still persisted. Both land acts in fact had included a clause allowing land purchase – where the government would buy the land off the landlord to sell to the tenants who would repay in instalments over a fixed period of time, much like a house mortgage today. This smart idea had originated with the nationalist Fintan Lalor in the 1840s and been taken up by English radicals such as John Stuart Mill and John Bright. Gladstone, however, believed in the innate virtues of landlordism, if only Irish landlords could be persuaded to act as model Englishmen, and was reluctant to adopt this method, emasculating it by demanding large deposits before the borrowing could start. Hence few tenants took up the offer.

The Tories were quicker to grasp the potential popularity of land purchase and the fact it not only offered the government a way out of the morass of land agitation, but threw a lifebelt to their allies, the landlords. Rents had become increasingly difficult to collect, and there was in any case a European-wide agricultural depression. In extreme cases agents had been peppered with gunshot, landlords faced with symbolic graves dug outside their front doors, or the whole estate boycotted – the word itself coming from its first application against Captain Boycott, Lord Erne's agent in Roscommon. The chance to sell up, if not sell out and leave Ireland, must have come as a relief to many of the gentry class.

By a series of radical land acts, starting in 1885, driven home by the massive Wyndham Act of 1903, and completed by the 1909 act, British governments revolutionised the business of landholding in Ireland. Landlordism was wound up and rural Ireland became a nation of owner occupiers. The Land Question truly was solved.

Of the two camps within Ireland under consideration in this chapter, the unionists and nationalists, the former had lost many of their traditional distinguishing characteristics by 1904. The Anglo-Irish ascendancy, in literal terms the owners of Ireland, were on the way out. No longer was it possible to meet superb grotesques such as the third Earl of Kingston who commissioned Mitchelstown Castle in County Cork stipulating it should be bigger than any other house in Ireland and ready to receive George IV on his next Irish visit. The King never came but that did not stop 'Big George' from entertaining on a regal

Cead Mile Failte, *a hundred thousand welcomes, for King Edward VII as he comes ashore from a summer cruise along the Irish west coast in 1903. He had also received a great welcome on his first visit as a young officer in the Grenadier Guards from an actress named Nellie Clifden, smuggled into his quarters at the Curragh by sympathetic brother-officers. However, in 1885 at the height of Parnell's drive for Home Rule, he met with crowds waving black flags and black handkerchiefs, booing and even throwing onions. The Prince's equerry wrote to Queen Victoria: 'the lower classes, the lazzaroni of Cork … were rabid rebels.'*

scale. The end came when his ungrateful tenants failed to vote for his candidate in the 1830 election. They were summoned to meet their landlord in the great gallery of the Castle; duly turned up; and then witnessed the earl shrieking to himself and going off his head in spectacular style. Commenting on this event, the novelist Elizabeth Bowen (her people being north Cork neighbours of the Kingstons) put her finger on the significance of his demise. 'The sense of dislocation was everywhere.

Property was still there, but power was going. It was democracy, facing him in his gallery, that sent Big George mad.'

Democracy continued its advance throughout the 19th century at the expense of the ascendancy. For George Moore the watershed came after the 1870 land act. Before then 'Ireland was feudal, and we looked upon our tenants as animals that lived in hovels round the bogs, whence they came twice a year with their rents.' For Martin Ross, one half of the writing part-

Punchestown, April, 1913. *The Countess of Arran (centre) with friends at the Kildare Hunt Steeplechases. Enviable hats are worn by both men and women.*

Flat shooting caps *more in evidence (right) in a family scene on the steps of Clonbrock House, County Galway, at the turn of the century. Lord Clonbrock (standing left) was a keen photographer himself, as were his children. One of his daughters, Miss Ethel Dillon, lived on alone at Clonbrock House, after the death of her brother, the last Lord, in 1926. Well into her eighties, she would hold morning prayers in the hall, for herself and the butler, just the two of them; they sang hymns and took it in turn to play the organ.*

nership of Somerville and Ross, the secret ballot act of 1872, which prevented landlord pressure at elections, served as the dividing line.

The land purchase acts completed the transformation of the Anglo-Irish from lords of creation to a socially exclusive minority, clinging to the Big House, some ludicrous, some admirable. Many struggled to keep up appearances, and the measures taken were sometimes desperate. The fourth Earl of Kingston, son of Big George, was wiped out by a financial crash but, with his gallant house party, he barricaded the doors to the castle and withstood a siege of bailiffs and creditors for a fortnight. At Menlough Castle in County Galway, Sir John Blake became an MP partly to obtain immunity against his creditors; when elected his constituents reported to the adjacent river where their landlord and new MP was sitting in a boat to avoid the bailiffs waiting for him on the bank. Also in County Galway stood Tyrone House, another great stone pile, but by the late 19th century its owners, the St George family, were reduced to squatting in various corners of the dilapidated mansion, cooking being done on an open fire in the top room. Other Anglo-Irish families who exchanged their estates for cash

through the land acts, including the 12 per cent additional payment known as the Bonus, enjoyed temporary affluence in the early 1900s, a modest number embellishing their houses or even building anew. Less pragmatic types blew their windfall on the gaming tables, one Irish peer ecstatically greeting George Wyndham, the Chief Secretary for Ireland, at Monte Carlo by pointing to his chips and crying 'George, George, the Bonus!'

Even when functioning normally, Irish country houses were marked by various inconveniences. Many were notoriously cold; a resourceful visitor to Lord Drogheda's house once arrived with a heavy trunk which, when the footmen were hauling it upstairs, burst open revealing it to be entirely filled with coal. The servant problem reared its head repeatedly, exacerbated by the custom of recruiting the upper servants from England, but 'the good ones won't come to Ireland'. The turnover could be rapid, and those that stayed on sometimes startled guests: 'the head housemaid looked like an elderly caricature of Disraeli in his later days.' Sanitation could be rudimentary. Bowen's Court had no bathroom until the 1930s; at Cahirnane in Kerry those wishing to use the lavatories found

them to be a row of eight huts, 'beginning with a giant-sized one down to one for a dwarf or infant', amidst the dripping laurels. An old man with an umbrella would accompany ladies and then insist on waiting for them lest they got wet on the return journey.

Although there was a vigorous social season in Dublin from January to mid March, based around the Castle – 'we were almost as magnificent as Buckingham Palace with our toy court' – grander gentry deserted the land for the subsequent London season and more exotic destinations. Trinity College, Dublin, continued as the Anglo-Irish university, but its graduates now tended to move abroad to England or the Empire. Ireland became the nursery, summer holiday house, and eventual old folks' home. Gentry politics remained unionist, but the small number of protestants in the south – 250,000 amongst two and a half million catholics – spread out over a large area, meant representative extinction in the harsh world of universal suffrage. A ginger group, the Irish Loyal and Patriotic Union, formed in 1885, did its best to influence public opinion throughout the three southern provinces – but to little avail.

A fine threnody for the Anglo-Irish country gentry appears at the end of *Bowen's Court*, Elizabeth Bowen's book about her family and family home:

> In the main I do not feel that they require defence – you, on the other hand, may consider them indefensible. Having obtained their position through an injustice, they enjoyed that position through privilege. But, while they wasted no breath in deprecating an injustice it would not have been to their interest to set right, they did not abuse their privilege – on the whole. They honoured, if they did not justify, their own class, its traditions, its rule of life. If they formed a too grand idea of themselves, they did at least exert themselves to live up to this: even vanity involves one kind of discipline. If their difficulties were of their own making, they combatted these with an energy I must praise. They found no facile solutions; they were not guilty of cant. Isolation, egotism and, on the whole, lack of culture made in them for an independence one has to notice because it becomes, in these days, rare.

Elsewhere throughout most of Ireland, unionism was confined to the larger towns and cities, the professional men and the

Lugubrious terriers *and a more assured child, all dressed up, in the Hughes family's pony trap in front of Dalchoolin House, Holywood, Belfast, in 1908. The Anglo-Irish delight in horses and animals in general was endless. The Beresford brothers of Curraghmore, County Wexford, rode a pig down Piccadilly* *and took a favoured horse upstairs to their mother's bedroom. Arthur MacMorrough Kavanagh, a popular Carlow landlord, would receive his tenants on a fine day sitting beneath an oak tree in the courtyard of his mansion, dressed in a black cloak, with his pet bear in attendance.*

bigger industries. There was, however, one very obvious region soaked to the pores with aboriginal unionism, from the upper to the lower classes, embracing all of the protestant persuasion – the north-east counties of Ulster.

Ulster was British, as the saying went. From the 17th-century plantation the place had filled with English and Scottish families, the local inhabitants being pushed into the less profitable upland areas. The newcomers were protestants, of course, but the Scotch element introduced the Calvinist strain of Presbyterianism – an ideal religion for an embattled, besieged people. Although the settlers fought together against catholic revanchism in the later 17th century, they were not always comfortable with each other. In particular the nonconformists suffered as second-class citizens, unable to enter the closed world of Anglican power and influence. Such discrimination had led some of their leaders to join with catholic dissidents in the risings against the British government in the late 18th century, most famously in 1798. Unlikely action from future unionists, one might think – but the protestant component of the rebels was never entirely happy with the catholic element, and the old sectarian division soon resumed its sway, best symbolised by another, very different Ulster movement founded in the same 1790s – the Orange Order.

Loyalty on wheels, *celebrating the coronation of George V in 1911. It was a Belfastman, John Boyd Dunlop, who invented the pneumatic tyre in Belfast in 1889, thereby freeing a whole new social class, not least women. (Dunlop features in Stewart Parker's delightful first play* Spokesong, *while black, solid bicycles demonstrate the horrific atomic theory in Flann O'Brien's* The Third Policeman.*) Recently, Ireland has produced international cyclists, such as Sean Kelly and the Tour de France winner Stephen Roche.*

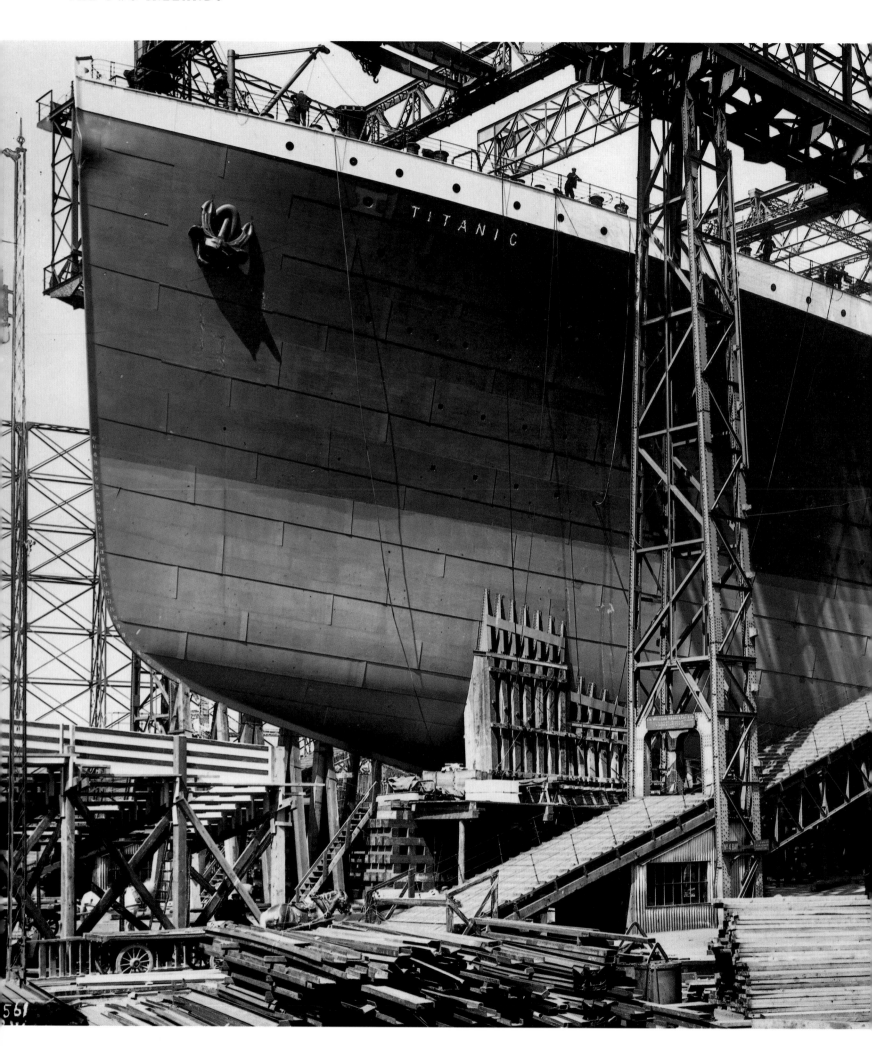

'Even the Pope couldn't sink her' *yelled an exuberant fitter at the launch of the* Titanic *from Belfast in 1911. At that date the city had the largest shipyards in the world – testament to resourceful entrepreneurs and cheap labour, since all coal and iron had to be imported. Workers in the shipyards were almost exclusively protestant. As the number of catholic immigrants grew, especially after the Famine, sectarian riots periodically erupted (in 1857, 1864 and 1886) over the question of employment and related issues. The other great industry in the north was linen, epitomised by this Belfast linen factory, above, in 1911. The Huguenots, protestant religious refugees from France, had developed this textile manufacture in the Lagan valley in the late 17th century. Linen remained the bedrock of Ulster's prosperity until the early 20th century.*
[PHOTO, ABOVE: ALEXANDER HOGG]
[PHOTO, LEFT: R. WELCH]

Sectarian fear of catholicism joined with a sense of racial superiority and a belief that the northern protestants' way of life would be ruined by incorporation into any self-governing Irish institution run from Dublin. The north-east had witnessed the only real industrial development in Ireland – Belfast its only industrial city. It became a major shipbuilding centre in the 1850s, which in turn led to the development of engineering and ropeworks. By 1900 it was a city of 400,000, from a town of 19,000 a century before. Much of the north's industry was geared to external, Empire markets and any possible commercial threat – say protectionism from a Home Rule government – therefore to be resisted.

But Ulster was not an integral unit: alongside the 900,000 protestants were 700,000 catholics. Belfast had a substantial catholic minority, packed into sharply defined districts; while Ulster's second city Derry (named Londonderry by the planters) had an overall catholic majority, though the city's institutions remained under the control of protestants.

As the Home Rule movement picked up pace, so too did Ulster protestant opposition. It was no coincidence that there was virtually no land war in the north, where in any case relations between landlord and tenant had always been fairly amicable. Riots broke out in 1886 over the Home Rule crisis – partly sparked in Belfast by a tactless catholic who pointed out

Physical force nationalists. *(Left) James Daly, a moving spirit in the the Land League; (centre) Tom Clarke and (right) Sean MacDermott, both of the IRB and both to be executed in 1916.*

Emigrants. *(Left to right) Oscar Wilde, whose reputation has risen, G. B. Shaw, now in eclipse, and James Joyce, who only ever left Ireland in a physical sense.*

There have always been two strands to Irish political nationalism: the constitutional, and the physical force element. The former would desire autonomy for Ireland, some welcoming a federal solution as with Home Rule, others perhaps going further towards separation; but the *method* must remain the same, that of peaceful persuasion exercised through the official channel of parliamentary politics. The latter rejected constitutional methods as ineffective and argued for an armed uprising by the Irish people. Their aim, too, was more extreme: a complete break with Britain and hence the establishment of an Irish republic.

The republican movement could trace back its origin to the late 18th century and the days of the French Revolution. An independent Irish republic achieved by force of arms had been the aim of the United Irishmen in 1798; and similar movements would break out time and again throughout the 19th century and on into the 20th. Indeed it is still the basic aim of the physical force men active in the North of Ireland today.

Until the 20th century such risings had been failures, but they served to become beads on the rosary of advanced nationalists: 1798 and the United Irishmen, 1803 and Robert Emmet, 1848 and Young Ireland, 1867 and the Fenians. The last group had been founded as the Irish Republican Brotherhood, the IRB, in 1858. By 1900 it seemed as if the physical force men had had their day. After the failed uprising of 1867, the Fenians had moved closer to a compact with the constitutional nationalists at Westminster. In the 1880s large elements of the movement (the very nature of the society meant it could never be an homogenous body) had been captured by Parnell, mesmerised by his masterly control and rhetorical ambiguities – occasionally speaking the language of Fenianism (especially in America) but practising legal action. Parnell's achievement had been to combine the two strands of Irish nationalism and form an Irish parliamentary party at Westminster backed by massive popular support throughout Ireland. Nationalist men of violence still exercised their option, but in an isolated fashion. The Invincibles assassinated the Chief Secretary in 1882 – cutting his throat with six-inch surgical knives, to the fascinated horror of the newspapers – while rogue dynamiters attempted, fruitlessly, to blow up London Bridge, various London stations and other imperial targets in the early 1880s. The majority of Fenians, however, were content to march with the Chief, happy to believe that his Home Rule goal masked a stepping stone to separation.

Parnell led his party throughout the 1880s, winning the

that protestants might no longer hold a monopoly of certain jobs in the shipyards, but also by a common, and mysterious, belief that the Royal Irish Constabulary were catholic hitmen from the south charged with the duty of shooting down the protestants. Thirty-two people were killed in the riots that summer, a figure not exceeded until the 20th century.

At Westminster, political allegiances rapidly polarised. The Irish Liberals vanished in the 1880s, while the Conservatives subsumed Major Saunderson and his unionists. In May 1886 there was talk even of armed resistance to the imposition of Home Rule: Saunderson announced the preparation of an army of 100,000 men and the likelihood of General Lord Wolseley and one thousand defecting British officers leading them. Unlike Ulster's agitations in 1914, most of this was little more than a facade – but it marked the strengths and depths of unionist feeling there. There was to be no gentlemanly ILPU for the northerners.

In the early 20th century then, one part of Ireland was decidedly non nationalist and committed to the unionist cause. Its social leaders might be drawn from the old Anglo-Irish families, but the land acts had plucked their estates from them. The real economic and hence political strength of unionism lay with the hardfaced men in the north. The rest of Ireland – the decisive majority – can safely be described as nationalist in 1900. In political terms, this meant a wish for greater self government; in cultural terms, the belief that Ireland deserved a separate identity distinct from the English public and its tastes.

prize of Gladstone's conversion to Home Rule in 1886. Parnell's personal downfall in 1891 was on an operatic scale: cited in a divorce case, rejected by his Liberal allies, then his own party and the bulk of Irish opinion; hounded by the Church; driven to his grave. But the disaster, although severely damaging, did not wreck the constitutional nationalists. Following hallowed Irish custom, the party split, with the minority of MPs following Parnell, yet eventually the division was healed in 1900 under the leadership of John Redmond. Their policy now was to wait for a Liberal administration, and then remind the government of Mr Gladstone's pledge.

The IRB continued its shadowy existence (its numbers of course impossible to determine), while other fringe republican organisations began to appear. The Boer War, with its first indications of cracks in the Empire's structure. encouraged such resistance. One of this new brood was titled Sinn Fein, founded in 1906 by the journalist Arthur Griffith, advocating a loosely defined national independence to be achieved by an interesting abstentionist policy – the simple removal of Irishmen from British institutions, not least Parliament. But the total impact of all such splinter groups remained negligible compared to the political weight of the constitutional nationalists, their policies and tactics unchanged since the 1880s.

Where nationalism did develop and change at a great rate was in the cultural field. From the early 1890s to the Great War intense literary activity pulsated around Ireland, in Dublin, naturally, but also Connaught in the west of Ireland. The fundamental aim was to assert the separate identity of Ireland by making the people conscious they were heirs to an ancient civilisation.

The process had three ingredients – partly complementary, partly antagonistic. First off was the hunt for an Irish literature distinct from British, London-based concerns. This Irish Literary Renaissance, as it was dubbed, concentrated on Irish themes and style but through the medium of the English language. The Irish language, Gaelic, had died out shortly after the Great Famine, its use associated with poverty and humiliation. Now in the 1890s came a scholarly interest in a revival of the language, the second ingredient. Dovetailing with this concern was the third ingredient: the general, more popular rediscovering of ancient Irish games, clothes and customs.

Undeniably the man most associated with the first group, the Anglo-Irish literary movement, was the poet, W.B. Yeats. It was Yeats who founded the Irish Literary Society in London where he was living, in 1891, and the National Literary Society in Dublin the next year. It was Yeats who dominated the core of the literary group, comprising Lady Gregory, AE (the nom de plume of George Russell), J. M. Synge, George Moore and Edward Martyn. James Joyce was definitely not a member of this movement; at bottom, he said, he distrusted all enthusiasm. Oscar Wilde and George Bernard Shaw, long resident in England, had little contact with the Renaissance; neither did the unionists, Somerville and Ross, authors of that masterly dissection of the Anglo-Irish world, *The Real Charlotte*.

The group produced plays, poetry and many essays in the pursuit of 'the Irish mind'. Synge was the only first-class dramatist of the group, although his plays were outnumbered by Lady Gregory's, sometimes written by herself, sometimes in collaboration with Yeats. Her true value was as an enthusiast and organiser of the group, and supporter of impecunious literati. George Moore did once collaborate with Yeats over a play on the legend of Diarmuid and Grania. The plan was that Moore should write the play in French, Lady Gregory translate it into English, Taidgh O Donoghue translate it into Irish, for Lady Gregory to translate it back into English and finally Yeats to apply the stylistic polish. Moore did write at least one act in French and published it at the end of his autobiographical volume *Ave* (the stage directions open with '*une caverne*'), if only , as he claimed, to 'convince the reader that two such literary lunatics as Yeats and myself existed, contemporaneously'.

George Moore was a cultural exile, from an Irish gentry (yet catholic) background. Most of his life was spent in Paris and London, but he did return to Dublin from 1901 to 1910 and left a splendidly sardonic account of the whole process in *Ave,* and its two sequels *Salve* and *Vale*. Eventually he fled Ireland once more: 'Ever since I have been in the country I have heard people speaking of working for Ireland … vainly sacrificing all personal achievements, humiliating themselves before Ireland as if the country were a God … And I began to tremble lest the terrible Cathleen Ni Houlihan might overtake me. She had come out of that arid plain, out of the mist, to tempt me, to soothe me into forgetfulness that it is the plain duty of every Irishman to dissociate himself from all memories of Ireland – Ireland being a fatal disease, fatal to Englishmen and doubly fatal to Irishmen.'

Edward Martyn was another playwright involved with the founding of the Abbey Theatre – what became, in effect the national theatre of Ireland – along with Yeats and Lady Gregory. (There was some contention over who was the main founder.) It was an excited Martyn, fresh from observing a production of Yeats' *The Countess Cathleen*, who, according to Moore, telegraphed Moore with the message, 'The sceptre of intelligence has passed from London to Dublin.' Last of the group was AE, a minor poet, but effective journalist and unique in literary Dublin in being loved by almost all contemporaries. AE's own definition of a literary movement was five or six people who live in the same town and hate each other cordially.

Essentially the group, particularly during the early years, felt that imagination was superior to reason. Hence their interest in occultism, magic, fairies and folklore. 'G. Russell's chief word is "opalescent" and we waited, intent, till it should appear. Appear it did within five minutes, and then in every second sentence ... It is, apparently, the colour of all visitants from the spiritual world.' Such preoccupation led sometimes to a confusion between lecturer and audience. Yeats recalled his first address to the Irish Literary Society in London as being on the theme

William Butler Yeats, *the image of The Poet with tousled hair, pince-nez, extravagant bowtie, in about 1900. An American journalist wrote at about this time of his face being 'as plastic to mood or emotion as an actor's … and magnetism of a delicate nervous sort was in his face as well as in his words and the swift angular gestures that went with them.' Above is his invaluable colleague and patron, Lady Gregory, whose practical nature helped the Abbey Theatre to survive its early years.* [PHOTOS, LEFT AND ABOVE: G. C. BERESFORD]

of 'the falling asunder of the human mind'. One of that audience, many years later, remembered Yeats giving a talk about fairies, mostly County Sligo fairies. Much of the hocus pocus – gyres, great wheels, cabala and the like – belonged to Yeats' distinctive concerns, but the group's preoccupation with mysticism led them burrowing back to the Celtic legends, especially that of Cuchulainn, the hero of Ulster – Gaelic Ulster. Such emphasis from the hands of mesmeric writers was to have a profound influence on the younger generation.

Irish dancing, Irish sport. *A display of the former in County Antrim, 1900. Stepdancing can be traced back to the 18th century; in the 1890s the Gaelic League popularised and promoted this indigenous Irish activity – fast, intricate footwork, with the arms motionless. On the right Kilkenny boys with hurley sticks in the 1920s. Despite the anglicisation of Irish life after the 17th century, hurling had continued, especially in the south, and was given a new lease of life by the founding of the Gaelic Athletic Association by Michael Cusack in 1884.* [PHOTO, LEFT: FRANCIS J. BIGGAR] [PHOTO, RIGHT: FR. BROWNE S. J.]

The second strand of cultural nationalism belonged to Douglas Hyde and the Gaelic League, founded in Dublin in 1893. Its aim was the preservation of Irish (Gaelic) as the national language; and the related study of literature in Irish. Enthusiasm for Irish began to grow, slowly in the 1890s, then with a rush in the 1900s, especially amongst the educated urban folk. The writer Sean O'Faolain remembers the intoxicating thrill of diving into this private pool of secret language. The conversion was accompanied by changing his birth name, John Whelan, to the Irish form – a process adopted by similarly enthused young men and women in the early twentieth century. It became the fashion to address letters in Irish, to the initial mystification of the Post Office. Irish titles, signs, catchphrases began to appear. Finally, in 1909, Hyde managed to make Irish a compulsory subject for matriculation at the new National University.

Hyde, himself a protestant, was emphatic that the Gaelic League should be non-sectarian, and indeed apolitical. During the early years both protestants and catholics were members. But protestant enthusiasts tended to be from the gentry class outside the north-east, and their invocation of a new Ireland peopled by noble aristocrats, and even more noble peasants, had very little appeal to working-class protestants in Belfast. Soon the Gaelic movement began to be captured by those who felt that

an organisation to promote Irish nationality had to be political.

Such a concern merged into a general belief that all aspects of Irish life should be purged of English pollutants. Foremost amongst these contaminating influences were games not indigenous to ancient Irish society. These were defined by Archbishop Croke as 'foreign and fantastic field sports, such as lawn tennis, polo, cricket, croquet' and we can add rugby and soccer. True Irishmen should play the national sports of hurling and Gaelic football (the latter hard to find amongst the records of early Irish society). Michael Cusack founded the Gaelic Athletic Association (GAA) to promote these. Not only were GAA members forbidden from playing these foreign games, even watching them was not to be tolerated. (This sporting apartheid continued until the 1970s, though inevitably much honoured in the breach.) Cusack was a large, bulky man, invariably clad in Irish tweeds, with a blackthorn stick and a big dog. He liked to call himself the Citizen and as such has been immortalised as the bullying nationalist in the Cyclops section of *Ulysses*: 'There's the man, says Joe, that made the Gaelic sports revival … So off they started about Irish sport and shoneen games the like of the lawn tennis and about hurley and putting the stone and racy of the soil and building up a nation once again and all of that.' The GAA clearly had political inclinations towards the advanced nationalists. At Parnell's funeral in 1891, 2,000 GAA men had marched with draped hurley sticks.

In the early 1900s the equation began to develop that to be an authentic nationalist one had to be an Irish speaker – and catholic to boot. George Moore was told, 'Plunkett is a Protestant, and a Protestant can never know Ireland.' The literary movement – Yeats and company – opposed this tendency vehemently. All of them, including Lady Gregory and Synge who could translate Irish, realised that English had now become the mother tongue of almost all the island. They believed in Home Rule, supporting the Irish party at Westminster, but recoiled from the hijacking of the cultural renaissance by extreme nationalists. Only J. M. Synge was unusual in seeming indifferent to all political solutions. His brother once wrote of him: 'He wished to see [Ireland's] people better and happier, but he did not feel very sure how these conditions were to be brought about.'

As far as the advanced men were concerned, histories were to be ransacked, ancient manuscripts discovered, new plays

and poems written – but only victories, glorious deeds and honours should be paraded before the public. In 1899 Yeats got into trouble with his play *The Countess Cathleen* by depicting peasants in what was seen by the newly middle-class Abbey audience as a patronising way. In fact Yeats' own attitude was by no means arrogant – quite the reverse. His view was fundamentally romantic: the Irish peasant was the noble savage figure, full of innocence, genius and poetry, untouched by corrupt civilisation. His mutterings were proverbs of wisdom, his songs the venerable chants of the fili – the singing poets of old. Soon the Dublin theatre audience would begin to rate Yeats' and Lady Gregory's plays according to a ration of PQ: peasant quality. But in *The Countess Cathleen* Yeats made the mistake of portraying both good and bad peasants.

Yeats did redeem his reputation among the advanced nationalists by his play *Cathleen ni Houlihan*. It was produced in 1902 specifically for Maud Gonne – Yeats' great but unrequited love, and a passionate nationalist, who played the title role. The message of the play seemed to be that young men must be ready to be summoned to die for Ireland. Yeats' mystical, flamboyant lines had a profound effect on the entire gamut of nationalist opinion. Even staid constitutional Home Rule supporters were moved. 'I went home asking myself', said one of these men, Stephen Gwynn, ' if such plays should be produced unless one was prepared for people to go out to shoot and be shot.' Many years later, after the 1916 rising, Yeats asked himself the same question:

> Did that play of mine send out
> Certain men the English shot?

This is a reminder (*pace* W. H. Auden) that poetry does sometimes make things happen. Various republicans thought the play 'a sort of sacrament'; 'sort of gospel'. After 1916 Yeats makes Patrick Pearse, one of the rising's leaders, acknowledge the necessity of a blood sacrifice in his poem 'The Rose Tree'.

Cathleen ni Houlihan, however, was the last piece of work of which contemporary nationalist Dublin approved. From then on the literary movement and the proponents of Irish Ireland went increasingly different ways. The reception of Synge's plays illustrates the real division. The first of his two controversial plays was the less well known *In the Shadow of the Glen* produced in 1903. Here Synge depicts the loneliness and frustration of a young woman married to an old man, a fate fairly common in rural Ireland until recently. At the end of the play she elopes with a fellow more her age. It is sensitively handled, with the sexual element left implicit. There was an outcry from the nationalists. Such things could not happen in holy Ireland. The head of Sinn Fein declared the play to be false: the eloping wife was a lie, he said, ' because all of us know that Irish women are the most virtuous in the world.'

Yet the hostility shown to this play was nothing compared to what greeted *The Playboy of the Western World*, produced in 1907. Essentially this play offended opinion in the same way as *The Countess Cathleen*: that is it showed peasants as earthy,

non-idealised human beings, who laughed, swore and mentioned ladies' garments such as a shift. Lady Gregory's telegram to Yeats, then in London, ran as follows: 'Audience broke up in disorder at word shift STOP What should I do?' Yeats telegraphed back: 'Leave it on'. Still the demonstrations and counter demonstrations continued: shouts of disapproval throughout the play; drunken Trinity College students riposting with God Save the King. After his rapid return to Dublin, Yeats strode forward to the front of the stage to remonstrate in vain with the protesters. (He was to tussle again with an Abbey audience in the 1920s over O'Casey's *The Plough and the Stars* when there was a frightful outburst because the men of 1916 were not receiving the full heroic treatment. This time Yeats announced his disgust with the audience by a dramatic opening: 'You have disgraced yourselves *again*', as if addressing the very same house; it had no more effect than on the first occasion.) The maddened Abbey theatregoers never forgave Synge for letting Ireland down, as they saw it, by portraying the western peasantry as comic hicks, so that the English – oh God forbid – so that the English might laugh condescendingly at those amusing little Irish folk.

For Yeats and company, the Playboy riots marked the split between the literary movement and the culturally conservative middle-class nationalists. Yet the irony is that Yeats and company were in part responsible for the growth of such nationalism. They were the ones who turned Irish minds in the 1890s back towards Ireland and the search for its separate culture. By 1907 the genie they had released had escaped from their control. The journalist, A. P. Moran, for instance, by inspired use of nicknames such as 'sour-faces' for protestants, 'west-Brits' for the Anglo-Irish – a term so successful in the suggestion of twit for Brit than it can still be heard today – and 'shoneens' for those native catholic Irish who aped British fashions, exacerbated the Anglophobic element. By such ridicule, and constant sniping at the constitutional party at Westminster, Moran

The double life *of Constance Gore-Booth, Countess Markievicz. She was the eldest daughter of an Anglo-Irish baronet, privately educated at Lissadel, the family home in County Sligo, presented at Court in 1887 and thoroughly at home in the world of balls and levees. Then in 1900 she married a Polish Count, settled in Dublin in 1903 and began to move towards feminism, socialism and extreme nationalism, much to the distress of early admirers such as Yeats. Her last ball at Dublin Castle was in 1908; later an acquaintance asked whether she enjoyed going there, and she replied, 'No, I want to blow it up.' At left we see her with fellow cultural enthusiasts wearing kilts. In the 1916 rising she fought with the Irish Citizen Army and initially was condemned to death. In the 1918 General Election she became the first woman MP but declined to take her seat, in accordance with Sinn Fein policy. Imprisoned again during the war of independence, 'the rebel countess' completed her long journey from her background by branding the Anglo-Irish treaty of 1921 a betrayal of republican hopes.*

helped to discredit the cause of moderate Home Rule in the eyes of good nationalist Irishmen. Ultimately all this aided the rise of Sinn Fein, though it has to be emphasised that before the war this tiny association was no more than one of many nationalist groups, none with a seat in parliament.

W. B. Yeats' vision of Ireland was as a storehouse of symbols; but now he found them plundered by others who gave them a value somewhat different from what he had intended. In 1913 he ended his collection of poems entitled *Responsibilities* with 'A Coat':

I made my song a coat
Covered with embroideries
Out of old mythologies
From heel to throat;
But the fools caught it,
Wore it in the world's eyes
As though they'd wrought it.
Song, let them take it,
For there's more enterprise
In walking naked.

Intrepid motorists *in 1908: reliability trials conducted by the Irish Automobile Club. Mr W. F. Pearce pilots car number 65, a 35/45 hp Gladiator – its name redolent of the pioneering days of the internal combustion engine. Timekeepers Messrs Straight and Ebblewhite monitor the performance. There was no shortage of helpers when difficulties occurred. Cultural nationalism might have been growing at the turn of the century, but for many in Ireland the future was more material. 'The cars came scudding in towards Dublin, running evenly like pellets in the groove of the Naas road,' James Joyce, from 'After the Race' in his collection of short stories,* Dubliners *(1914).*

CHAPTER TWO

HOME RULE DELAYED: THE ULSTER CRISIS, 1911-14

Shutting the stable door. *An apprehensive King's Own Scottish Borderer closing the barrack gates after men from his regiment had shot dead four civilians and wounded 38 others, on 26 July 1914 at Howth, just north of Dublin. Emulating the Ulster Volunteers at Larne three months earlier, the southern Irish Volunteers bought arms from dealers in Hamburg and had landed a portion of them at Howth. The gunrunners were met by Irish Volunteers who spirited the cargo away, outwitting the police and soldiers who had been summoned. Two discomfited companies of the King's Own Scottish Borderers were being marched back to their barracks followed by a taunting crowd which began to throw stones as the troops approached the quays at Bachelor's Walk. Major Haig ordered his rearguard to block the road and they then opened fire. Nationalist Ireland was outraged at what was perceived to be the contrast between this incident and government inaction over the Larne gunrunning, a grievance heightened by Balfour's casual reply to an Irish MP's demand for justice: 'there isn't enough justice to go round'.*

THERE WERE TWO DRAWBACKS TO THE ASSUMPTION that, once a Liberal government came back into power, then Home Rule would follow. The first was that his party had been less enthusiastic than Mr Gladstone in embracing Home Rule. Such reluctance was seen most starkly after 1906 when the Liberals won a massive majority against the Unionists. Since the Irish parliamentary party was not needed to reach a majority in the Commons, the pledge to introduce Home Rule could be pushed far down the agenda. Secondly, even if the Liberal government of the day got round to passing a Home Rule bill in the Commons, as it had in 1893, the bill would then be vetoed by the Lords – as happened in 1893. But in 1910 political circumstances ensured that the Irish nationalist MPs once again held the balance of power (as in 1886 and 1892) and the obvious price for them ensuring a Liberal majority was Home Rule. Furthermore after 1911 the House of Lords lost its power to veto bills, being allowed only to delay them for no more than three sessions. At long last it seemed that nothing could prevent the passing of Home Rule for Ireland.

Protestant Ulster had different ideas – as did that part of the British establishment represented by the Tory party and the Army. These three forces joined together to resist what they saw as the danger of Home Rule in an increasingly open, unconstitutional and illegal fashion. Britain came closer to a revolution during these years immediately before the First World War than at any time since the 17th century. It would have been a revolution, moreover, led from the top, a coup d'etat to preserve various social and political institutions against the wishes of the majority, democratically expressed through Parliament.

The actual nine-county province of Ulster was by no means all unionist. There was a 55 per cent protestant majority in the province (itself a meaningless unit except for sporting occasions) but they were concentrated in the four eastern counties. Geographically the province was split roughly half and half between the two confessions, with the western counties of Tyrone, Fermanagh, Donegal, Monaghan and Cavan having a catholic majority. Unionist solidarity expressed itself through the Orange Order, which consisted of two-thirds

'Strawboys' visit a bride *before her wedding in County Sligo, 1910. Whatever the stirrings in the body politic, the old ways went on. Strawboys were Irish equivalents of the many groups of mummers who went round acting out traditional plays and songs at Christmas and other times of the year in England. They expected to be rewarded with food and drink in return for the entertainment they offered. In Ireland there had also been a tradition of young, well-educated but homeless men looking for hospitality in return for music and song, which may also have lain behind the strawboys.*
[PHOTO: W. A. GREEN]

Gutting herring *on the quay for curing at Ardglass, County Down. At the turn of the century the industry had been revived, after a long fallow period, large herring fleets putting ashore at the two main bases of Ardglass and Howth, County Dublin. Fresh herring was delivered to British and Irish markets, cured herring exported to America and Europe. For a brief period there was plentiful employment and comparative prosperity; by the 1920s, however, the herring had all but gone.*

Belleek Potteries, *1905, County Fermanagh, adding handles to china baskets before firing. Established in 1863, Belleek was Ireland's answer to Royal Worcester china. The style of open fretwork baskets covered in delicate flowers and shells proved a must for Victorian collectors, and ensured Belleek's place in the pantheon of British china manufacturers. Their main market today is in the United States.*
[PHOTOS, LEFT AND ABOVE: W. A. GREEN]

of adult protestant males. (Catholics, of course, were not admitted, even assuming they might have wished to enter.) Religion, more than any other factor, was the badge of distinction between the two communities, since the catholics neither spoke a different language nor were of different pigmentation. The protestants felt themselves to be a superior people, a settler class and race far removed from the defeated Irish catholics, skulking in the poorer upland regions and practising an alien European religion. Resistance to Home Rule meant resistance to the Vatican's tentacles. 'Home Rule means Rome Rule' became the slogan of the day. Surrender to Home Rule ensured government by inadequates in Dublin. A popular cartoon showed the parliament house in Dublin amidst dirty, manure-strewn streets, with grass growing in the pavement and donkeys ties to lamp posts.

The Union was regarded as the sheet anchor for protestant superiority; but this did not mean Ulster Unionists felt Britain should be supported at all times. 'Loyalists' then, and now, agreed on loyalty to the Crown so long as the Crown safeguarded their interests – as defined by Ulstermen. Englishmen did not always warm to such distinctions – then as now. In the late 19th century *Punch* investigated this soi-disant term:

> *Loyal to whom, to what?*
> *To power, to pelf,*
> *To place, to privilege, in a word to self.*
> *Those who assume, absorb, control, enjoy all*
> *Must find it vastly pleasant to be loyal.*

Two Ulster Unionists, James Craig, later Lord Craigavon, and Major Crawford, later a gun-runner, declared that they would prefer to change their allegiance to the Emperor of Germany rather than be ruled by John Redmond.

In 1910 Sir Edward Carson became the leader of the Ulster Unionists. His grim-faced visage, reproduced in hundreds of press photographs over the next four years, encapsulated granite, protestant resistance. In some he strode along a street followed by adoring Ulstermen; in others his fists thumped the table at open air anti-Home Rule meetings; or his fingers pointed accusingly at government poltroons. There was not an ounce of compromise in his character or self-doubt amongst his beliefs. Although he exemplified everything protestant Ulster could want, strangely he was not from the North. He had been first a successful lawyer in Dublin, then London, and had only consented to lead the Ulster Unionists because without the North, Home Rule would, he imagined, be an impossibility. His aim, then, was not to separate Ulster from Ireland, but use the threat as blackmail to keep an undivided Ireland within the Empire. Ulster was an argument, not an end in itself.

In 1912 pressure was maintained by a pledge, portentously labelled by its framers as The Solemn League and Covenant; others affected an even more self-important title – the 'Sacramentum'. However pompous the language, the pledge

'What an awful face', *exclaimed a member of an ancient Irish family, Lady Fingall, on first glimpsing Sir Edward Carson. He is seen in characteristic mode (far left) and with a touch of modernity to his dress. MP for Dublin University, Carson was from the south, but took up the cause of Ulster in order to defeat that 'nefarious conspiracy' working for Home Rule. At his side is the Conservative leader, Andrew Bonar Law, Canadian-born but son of an Ulster Presbyterian minister. Tagging alongside Sir Edward, and with an apologetic face, he seems to justify Asquith's description of him as 'meekly ambitious'. He did supplant Lloyd George as prime minister in 1922 but died the next year and was buried in Westminster Abbey: 'the Unknown Prime Minister beside the Unknown Soldier'.*

The imposing bulk *of Captain James Craig (near, top right) housed a nimble mind and complete identification with his people. Son of a millionaire distiller from the north of Ireland, Craig had done well in the Boer War, and became an MP in 1906. More than the southerner Carson, he understood and organised Ulster resistance during the crisis years of 1912–14. He later became Northern Ireland's first Prime Minister and was created Lord Craigavon.*

Lord Kitchener of Khartoum *with the Countess of Iveagh at the Dublin Horse Show, 1912 (bottom right). Kitchener epitomised the British Army for the general public – hence the famous recruiting poster in 1914 with his accusing finger. Although born in Kerry, he would have agreed with the sentiments of the first Duke of Wellington, also born in Ireland: 'Sir, a man may be born in a stable and is not a horse!' Lady Iveagh's husband was head of the Guinness brewing dynasty.*

Home Rule ahoy. *The most vigorous supporter of it in the government was the First Lord of the Admiralty, Winston Churchill, here perched (left) precariously on something smaller than a battleship; beside him is Colonel Seely, the ineffable Secretary of State for War, before being sacked over the Curragh Incident when a number of cavalry officers in Ireland announced they would prefer to resign rather than be sent north to coerce Ulster.*

John Redmond, *below, far left, the Irish Nationalist leader in Parliament, about to emerge and claim his prize; his fate, in fact, was to witness the complete destruction of his constitutional party at the hands of Sinn Fein in the 1918 election. He died that same year and for long has been dismissed from the pageant of 20th-century Irish history; only recently have his vision and role been properly appreciated.*

Lord Aberdeen, *below, near left, the Viceroy appointed by the Liberals in 1906, and in fact resuming his post, since he had reigned briefly in Ireland in 1886. A genuine supporter of Home Rule, he and his wife spent much of their own money on good works, but they never enjoyed the approval of smart Ascendancy society. Lady Aberdeen towered over the small, bearded Lord Lieutenant, encouraging some to dub them Jumping Jack and Blowsy Bella. Lord Aberdeen was feared for his prowess at the Canadian polka – its steps unknown to the Dublin ton – and his chosen partner 'always had a "Heaven-help-me" look on her face'. Lady Aberdeen busied herself in philanthropic projects, the most important of which was her campaign against tuberculosis, though it has been said that her forceful publicity gave the unfortunate impression that everyone in Ireland was consumptive.*

was taken extremely seriously by the protestants in Ulster and no less than 471,444 men and women signed it, some reportedly using their blood as ink. The pledge committed signatories to oppose Home Rule, 'using all means which may be found necessary'. These were sometimes quite straightforward. The Earl of Antrim held a meeting to discuss the threat to the Union, at which he produced a revolver, placed it on the table before him and announced, 'anyone mentioning Home Rule will be shot!' There was a short silence and then the meeting broke up.

Reinforcements soon came from the Tories. Their support for the Ulster Unionists was not unexpected, of course: the Conservative party had added the Unionist name to its own after 1886 specifically on that issue. And in that year one of its maverick members, Lord Randolph Churchill, had gone to Belfast to excite the masses with fiery speeches and slogans such as 'Ulster will fight and Ulster will be right.' But the level of extra-parliamentary support, and particularly the sort of language used by His Majesty's Opposition, in England as well as Ulster during this later Ulster crisis, was to become quite extraordinary.

To an extent the Tories were seizing on Ulster as a stick with which to beat the Liberals: acceptable enough tactics from an opposition. Lord Randolph Churchill had said as much in a letter to a friend in 1886: 'If the GOM [Gladstone] goes for Home Rule, the Orange card would be the one to play. Please God it will turn out the ace of trumps and not the two.' Yet the Tory luminaries in 1912 – Andrew Bonar Law who succeeded Balfour as leader, and the new star of F. E. Smith, memorably described as having 'acquired, not diligently but with too much ease, the airs of a fox-hunting man who could swear elegantly in Greek' – went so far in their menacing phrases that it became more than a political manoeuvre. In June 1912 Bonar Law announced at a Unionist demonstration that 'there are things stronger than parliamentary majorities'. Next, the Conservative leaders met with their Ulster allies at an even larger assembly at Blenheim Palace (selected, perhaps, to annoy Winston Churchill, then in his Liberal phase and one of the few government ministers to sound determined over Home Rule). This time Bonar Law identified 'a corrupt parliamentary bargain' and then moved easily into undeniably seditious talk: the Ulster Unionists 'would be justified in resisting such an attempt [to impose Home Rule] by all means in their power, including force. I can imagine no length of resistance to which Ulster can go in which I should not be prepared to support them.' At the same meeting F. E. Smith publicly called to Sir Edward Carson to 'appeal to the young men of England!' In 1913 Lord Esher claimed that Ulster ought not to yield, 'even if a general election were to go in favour of the government'.

It is clear enough that emotional conviction had overtaken rational argument with the Tory–Ulster compact. An alliance between the majority in Parliament and the majority of Irish MPs was stigmatised as 'corrupt', but not an equivalent alliance

between respective minorities in the Commons and Ireland. The Ulster crisis touched an open nerve in the Establishment's body. In the early 20th century jingoism was at its height. There had been the nasty experience of the Boer War which suggested cracks in the structure of the Empire, and that meant men must rally round and support the flag. What was happening in Ireland, if unopposed, might spread to other parts. Rudyard Kipling was only one amongst many to produce stentorian verses promising succour to the loyalists in the North.

Back in 1886 there had been tentative arrangements for assembling the faithful and drilling them in military skills to oppose any imposition of Home Rule. The same now occurred on a most impressive scale. Orange parades had always featured drilled units and it proved to be an easy matter to extend this into a more formal protestant militia. Parade ground orders might be unconventional – one officer would halt his men by shouting 'Whoa' – but recruits were enthusiastic and determined. Various areas began to develop their own forces, the whole becoming the Ulster Volunteer Force from January 1913. As yet they had few arms but this defect was fast being remedied. Commanding them were various superannuated offi-

The King and all the King's horses. *George V and Queen Mary bask in Dublin's warm welcome, 1911. The 8th Irish Hussars lead his escort down Grafton Street (right). 'I was tremendously proud of belonging to the Empire, as were at that time most Irishmen', wrote*

Sean O'Faolain, born at the start of the century and an IRA member in the early 1920s. 'I gloried in all its trappings, Kings, Queens, dukes, duchesses, generals, admirals, soldiers, sailors, colonists and conquerors, the lot.'

cers from the regular Army, with the hearty approval of Field-Marshal Earl Roberts. And thus is introduced the second great ally (after the Tory party) which the Ulstermen enjoyed – the British military establishment.

The British Army at this time had many officers of Anglo-Irish stock – more in proportion than from any other part of the United Kingdom. Large numbers of these men came from the Ulster protestant community (a tradition continued during the Second World War, with commanders such as Montgomery, Alexander and Templer). Even those Army officers outside the Anglo-Irish world were instinctively behind the unionist cause, being naturally pro-Tory and pro-Empire.

Belfast children *play in the street (left) at the height of the General Strike.*

'PE and pumps' *for the girls (above) in the more refined surroundings of the National Ursuline Convent School in Waterford, 1908. The National schools were formed largely out of old village and town schools, many of which had been started and supported by the local landowning families.*

Eager Dublin crowds *await the arrival of the British Prime Minister, H. H. Asquith in July 1912 (left), an enthusiasm explained by his government's introduction of the Third Home Rule bill that April. A benign, rubicund Asquith tours an industrial school in Dublin (above), large number of clerics in attendance at a respectful distance. The next year the calm was broken by the Irish Transport and General Workers' Union strike over recognition of the union by William Martin Murphy's Tramway company. For eight months the Great Lock Out of 100,000 workers paralysed much of the economy, but in the end hunger forced the strikers' surrender. On the right, soldiers of the Connaught Rangers are put to work on the railways.* [PHOTO, RIGHT: FR. BROWNE S. J.]

Throughout the Ulster crisis, the Prime Minister and his cabinet, with the occasional exception of Winston Churchill, appeared like rabbits caught in the headlights of Sir Edward Carson's northern juggernaut. But as the crisis swelled during late 1913 and early 1914, some very senior officers decided to force the pace and compel the government to abandon any plans it might have to coerce Ulster. At the centre of these remarkable activities was General Sir Henry Wilson, a lanky framed and foxy faced Anglo-Irishman, Director of Military Operations at the War Office. He encouraged the Army command in Ireland, ineptly led by General Paget, to approach the equally inept Secretary of State for War, Colonel Seely, and extract a promise – a verbal promise with nothing in writing – that officers might be given the option of resigning their commissions rather than be sent north to coerce Ulster – whatever that meant. Paget returned to Ireland, hysterically lectured his officers on the situation as he saw it, which included a government 'plot' to suppress the Ulster Volunteers, and then awaited developments. (There existed, in fact, no official plan for suppression; any plot there was derived from the machinations of Wilson and his fellow cronies.) Immediately General Gough,

three colonels and fifty-five cavalry officers at the Curragh camp outside Dublin announced they would prefer dismissal rather than having to coerce Ulster; the next day this news was blazoned across the British press.

Whether this action qualifies as mutiny or not is beside the point. It is also irrelevant whether there was a government plan to move against the loyalists in Ulster. There should have been no Army discussion at all about future government business; its job was to do what elected politicians decided. After the Curragh incident, the government of the day could not rely upon the Army – the only means of taking action against the rebels in Ulster. When the news broke, the Prime Minister, Herbert Asquith, finally exerted himself, sacked Seely and two generals and took over the War Office personally. But Wilson was not removed; and nothing happened to the fifty-eight protesting officers at the Curragh – if anything their careers received acceleration in the years to come. One witness at the War Office, Major Archibald Wavell, later to become a distinguished commander in the Second World War, was appalled at Wilson's behaviour and flabbergasted at the lack of reaction from his political masters.

Socialism's messiah, *Big Jim Larkin, founder and leader of the Irish Transport and General Workers' Union, voice and arms extended, on his 'divine mission to create discontent'. Periodically imprisoned by the government during the strike, he managed to evade the police by wearing a false* *beard and so was able to address the faithful from the balcony of the Imperial Hotel in O'Connell Street on 31 August 1913 – quickly dubbed Bloody Sunday on account of police clubbing down people at the forbidden meeting (right). Four hundred, many just onlookers, were treated for wounds.*

Why did the government not attempt to meet the Army challenge head on? Partly it was pusillanimity at the top: Churchill appeared to be the only minister willing to fight, but because of his natural bellicosity rather than a love of Home Rule. Indeed few in England did genuinely accept Home Rule. Partly it was because of the sheer weight of the Establishment supporting the Unionists, from the Crown itself – there is evidence that King George V was sympathetic to the rebellious officers – to the whole formidable fabric of smart society. John Redmond said: 'The issue raised is wider even than Home Rule. It is whether the Government are to be browbeaten and dictated to by the drawing-rooms of London.' There was also, though, a growing realisation from some government quarters that perhaps the Ulster protestants did deserve separate treatment. At the beginning of his ministry Asquith was shackled to Redmond's Nationalist party, the price of which was Home Rule. Short of resignation, the Liberals had to persevere with it. Asquith accepted the line that Ulster's resistance was a bluff in 1911 and early 1912; but as the size and intensity of Ulster's reaction to the threat of Home Rule grew rather than evaporated, he began to listen to advocates of partition.

Perhaps Ulster, or parts of Ulster, could be excused from

Home Rule for a number of years, or maybe permanently? Unionists wanted permanent exclusion, of course; nationalists a limited number of years with the prospect of reunification. Horsetrading commenced over the projected boundary. Unionists pressed for the full nine counties; nationalists for the four with protestant majorities. The trouble was that nationalist minorities honeycombed those four north-eastern counties; likewise unionist minorities existed in the remaining counties, large ones in Tyrone and Fermanagh. When introduced in 1912, the Home Rule bill ignored any mention of a minority, although both Churchill and Lloyd George earlier had urged some element of exclusion. Gradually over the next two years Redmond was prevailed upon to accept temporary exclusion of four Ulster counties, a proposal snortingly rejected by Carson as merely a stay of execution of six years.

The impasse continued in 1914. The Ulster Volunteer Force was now matched by a similar force of Nationalist Volunteers in the south. The one declared itself ready to fight if Home Rule should come; the other if Home Rule was withdrawn. Presiding over the situation was the Chief Secretary for Ireland, Augustine Birrell. No Englishman greatly relished that appointment. When told of his new job by Campbell-Bannerman, the Prime Minister, in 1907, Birrell quickly suggested another name. 'Good heavens', the Prime Minster replied,' but he's a good friend of mine.' On his first official visit to Ireland, the captain of the mailboat had attempted to cheer up the sea-sick Birrell by remarking 'Chief Secretaries as

No fear to wear of '98. *Sombre faces, despite the flamboyant 1798 uniforms worn in memory of the rising against the British in that year, as this group of mourners returns from the funeral of those killed at Bachelor's Walk in Dublin, July 1914 (below). The southern Irish response to armed Ulstermen was to exchange such expressions of nationalism for a similarly armed volunteer force.*

Ulster will fight *is the message here as Sir Edward Carson presents 'colours' to the Ulster Volunteer Force in 1912 (above). The uniforms are leggings, flat caps and a variety of belts. In the background muster white-robed Volunteer nurses. Unionists could not see it, but they were making 'rebellion against the King, in the King's name'.*

a rule don't last long.' But Birrell did last, and also come to enjoy Ireland, especially Dublin and its literary excitements; his personal, if not political, inclination lay with the nationalists. Ulster unionists were 'devilish clever fellows, hard as nails and as sympathetic as rhinoceros … a people wholly untinged by romance.' His attitude to the state of affairs in 1914 was to take the tolerant approach and hope the fury might blow itself out.

As yet, neither nationalists nor unionists had the arms and munitions to sustain their boasts, though the UVF had been adept in acquiring a fair amount through unusual channels.

This situation was transformed in 1914 by a large-scale gun-running operation when, in a single night, the unionists landed plentiful supplies of arms purchased in Germany. The authorities made no attempt at any arrests. A gun-running escapade by the southern Volunteers was less well financed and on a much smaller scale, though carried out in broad daylight at Howth. Troops sent to prevent the landing failed in their mission, but managed to shoot dead some taunting bystanders. Although the Irish administration moved quickly to condemn this bloodshed, it seemed to many observers – and all national-

The Great War *now displaced purely Irish concerns. Along with the 36th (Ulster) division, two southern divisions were formed: the 10th and 16th (Irish) divisions. Officers of the Royal Dublin Fusiliers (above)* *prepare to depart for Gallipoli in 1915. In France, men from the same regiment proudly show off their collection of captured German arms and helmets.*

ist opinion in Ireland – that the government was not being evenhanded in its reaction to the respective militias.

Civil war moved a step closer, while at Westminster the Home Rule bill entered its final phase. In the summer of 1914 it passed the Commons for the third and last time, with an amendment allowing temporary exclusion for six years for the four Ulster counties with protestant majorities. This spirit of compromise was hardly echoed by the Lords, which promptly changed the amendment to permanent exclusion for all nine Ulster counties. In Belfast Carson's provisional government was in place to take over the province the moment Home Rule went on to the statute book. What saved Ireland – and quite possibly mainland Britain – from civil war in August 1914 was, of course, the greater war between nations in Europe. The third Home Rule bill, which had been so bitterly fought over since its inception, although formally passed, was suspended for the duration of hostilities.

At the other end of the world
*Antarctic exploration went on,
much of it featuring Ernest
Shackleton from a Kildare family.
As a junior officer he joined Scott's
first expedition and quickly made
his mark: Christmas Day, 1902
(top left), for the three-man sledge
journey over the Ross barrier:
from left to right, Lt Shackleton,*

*Capt Scott, Dr Wilson. Centre top,
Shackleton (right) leading his own
expedition on the Nimrod to
within 97 miles of the Pole in
1909; on his return he was lionised
and knighted. Top right, Sir Ernest
and Lady Shackleton on the
Endurance just before sailing in the
late summer of 1914. In the
Antarctic the ship was trapped and*

*eventually crushed by the ice
in 1915, a thousand miles from any
possible help. Shackleton then led
his crew over the ice to Elephant
Island, dragging with them sledges
and boats, and arriving in April
1916. From there the leader sailed
the 800 miles to South Georgia
with five others to bring help, in an
open 22-foot boat across the moun-*

*tainous seas of the southern ocean.
By August 1916 Shackleton
succeeded in rescuing the whole of
his party – and all this without
the slightest notion that Dublin
had been torn apart by the Easter
Rising or the war that would
be over by Christmas 1914 had
resulted in the greatest carnage
ever known.*

CHAPTER THREE

EASTER RISING, 1916

Children gathering firewood *from the Dublin rubble after the Easter Rising. J. P. Mahaffy, the Provost of Trinity College, Dublin, at this time, said that in Ireland the inevitable never happened, the unexpected always. To most in Britain and Ireland, the rising came out of the blue. To the many Irishmen fighting in France, the 1916 rising, involving 1,600 of their fellow countrymen, was a stab in the back. Mahaffy himself was well known for his taunts at the Nationalists, and during the week directed the defence of his College, which lay across the insurgents' strongholds. Patrick Pearse, the rising's leader, knew perfectly well that the campaign was a desperate throw, poorly supported, and likely to fail; but he banked on their sacrifice energising the national movement. His mentor could be said to be Ireland's mythical hero, Cuchulainn, whose saying was prominently displayed on the walls of St Enda's, the school founded by Pearse: 'I care not though I were to live but one day and one night, if only my fame and my deeds live after me.'*

THE RESPONSE FROM THE NORTH TO THE OUTBREAK of war was unambiguous, the Ulster Volunteers after all being in the business of defending the British Empire. Carson only argued for his men to be kept together, which was made possible with the creation of the Ulster Division. The proportion of Ulstermen who fought (and mostly died in July 1916 on the Somme) was higher than the rest of Ireland; though many from the south did volunteer, of course, being formed into two further Irish divisions, and demonstrating fighting qualities – not least the Munster Fusiliers and Dublin Fusiliers on V Beach at Gallipoli. By April 1916, 150,000 Irishmen were on active service. Yet in general southern Irishmen proved less enthusiastic about Belgium and 'the rights of small nations', believing that they also qualified as a nation deserving rights.

John Redmond, leader of the Irish parliamentary party, was a sincere nationalist and Home Ruler, but perhaps too much a 'good House of Commons man' – as Butt had been in the 1870s, and Parnell had definitely not been in the 1880s. He loved the institutions and customs of Westminster, and a substantial part of him felt loyal to Britain, especially in its hour of need. Home rule was on the statute book at last – if not yet implemented – and if nationalists proved themselves as willing to fight the new enemy as the northerners did, then a united Ireland might emerge. He quickly called for Irish volunteers to enlist for service in France and this provoked an inevitable split amongst the southern Volunteers, A dissident minority of about 10,000 out of 170,000 rejected any support for the British government, taking the old title of Irish Volunteers. Yet the great majority, now calling itself the National Volunteers, remained under Redmondite control. After the first flush, recruitment for France rapidly declined, however, and by the end of 1915 enthusiasm for the war was on the wane.

It was from the small force of Irish Volunteers that the Easter Rising sprang. Their leader, titled Chief of Staff, was Eoin MacNeill, Professor of History at University College, Dublin. But the real strength of the movement came from a secret inner circle, all members of the IRB – the old secret Fenian organisation sworn to establish the republic. Further to confuse matters, not all IRB men, not even the President of the Supreme Council of the IRB, were fully aware of the plans of this secret core, led by two younger IRB men, Sean MacDermott and Tom Clarke. (Fenian plots in the past had been so riddled with informers that secrecy even from other IRB men was thought paramount.) This splinter group formed itself into a secret military council and was to proclaim the Irish Republic in 1916.

'Through a sea crimson with blood' *charged the First Royal Munster Fusiliers on V Beach at Gallipoli in April 1915. To put ashore a large number of soldiers in a short time, an old collier, the* River Clyde, *was run aground and at 6.30 am troops rushed out of specially cut doors, along a flimsy catwalk and over a bridge of lighters. They ran straight into concentrated Turkish small-arms fire. About half the 2,000 soldiers aboard (Munster Fusiliers and the Hampshire Regiment) were cut down on the gangways or died in the water; the remainder stayed penned in the collier; a bare handful reached the shore and dug themselves in. One officer wrote, 'the dear men were just mown down in scores into a bloody silence'.*

One other force which became fully involved in the rising was James Connolly's Citizen Army. Connolly had founded the Irish Socialist Republican party in 1896 and until the First World War the socialist component appeared to be the more important for him. He had proved himself an able lieutenant to Big Jim Larkin, founder of the Irish Transport and General Workers' Union, and participated in his famous, but unsuccessful, struggle against that righteous spirit of capitalism – William Martin Murphy. With a gigantic presence and booming voice – 'you cannot argue with the prophet Isaiah', said one discomfited opponent – Larkin had taken on Murphy over recognition of his Union by Murphy's Tramway Company. Despite monster meetings, much agitation, and stoical hardship, the strikers were defeated in 1914. Larkin departed for America, but Connolly continued to organise in Ireland, and began to turn more towards Irish nationalism as a means of producing a socialist state. Larkin, like a good Marxist, believed in the internationalism of the working class and the false consciousness of national divides.

In 1914 then, Connolly's tiny Citizen Army (no more than 250 men) operated alone. As the war progressed, he became increasingly frustrated at the hesitancy of the Irish Volunteers, and started to think of independent military action. It was to prevent any precipitate outbreak that Connolly was invited to join the IRB in January 1916 and learn their plans for a rising on Easter Sunday, 23 April 1916.

England's war with Germany was seen as Ireland's opportunity. But MacNeill and the majority of the Irish Volunteers believed they had to wait for Irish opinion to agree with them before launching any attack. The inner core of IRB men rejected such comparatively careful tactics, and pressed on for a rising as soon as feasible. Who knew when the European war might finish and thus the moment pass? There was, moreover,

Regulation blackthorn *under his arm, an Irish Guards officer (left) talks to Rudyard Kipling towards the end of the war. After the loss of his Irish Guardsman son, Kipling wrote the history of the regiment in the war.*

'**My brave Irish**', *as Queen Victoria had once called her formidable Irish regiments. Irishmen from the south died in their thousands alongside their comrades from the north at the Somme in 1916. The most famous attack was by the 36th (Ulster) Division, which reached its objective 'in one of the finest displays of human courage in the world'. In just two days, 1–2 July, the division lost 5,500 men killed or wounded, and won four Victoria Crosses. But in addition to the 12 battalions of the 36th, 7 regular Irish battalions and 4 of Tyneside Irish were engaged that first day; later in the Somme campaign all three brigades of the 16th (Irish) division were prominent too. 'I looked around', recalled Rifleman Lucey of the Royal Irish Rifles, 'and saw all the Mac's and O's lying out there alongside the hardy Ulster boys. I was sick but proud.' The pictures of the Irish Guardsmen were taken by Fr. Frank Browne, one time regimental chaplain to the Irish Guards, and holder of the MC and Croix de Guerre.*
[PHOTOS, LEFT AND RIGHT: FR. BROWNE S. J.]

'**Known unto God**' *were Kipling's words for the individual gravestones and big memorials listing men who had died nameless or without trace. Stripped of salvageable boots, these bodies (right) await burial. They were probably all identifiable.*

the possibility of gaining German support – arms and munitions, perhaps even troops. The main advocate for this route was a most unlikely candidate: Sir Roger Casement, from an Ulster protestant family, knighted by Britain for his services exposing brutalities in Africa and South America. Casement's feelings for the underdog transferred themselves to his home country, and he had drunk so deep from the well of Irish nationalism that soon after the outbreak of war he conceived the scheme of working with Germany. Arthur Griffith and Sinn Fein had absolutely no inkling of any rising. Individual Sinn Feiners did take part in the rising, but only as Irish Volunteers or Citizen Army men. Those in the know were still a secret minority of the Irish Volunteers – itself a minority of the overall Volunteer movement.

The leaders of the rising had few illusions about the likelihood of military success. One of these men, Patrick Pearse,

made remarks in his prose and poetry almost welcoming failure, as the blood sacrifice required to invigorate moribund nationalism. Yeats' poem 'The Rose Tree' explicitly illustrates this.

There's nothing but our own red blood
Can make a right Rose Tree.

Undeniably there existed a strong romantic strain in some of the leaders of 1916: not just Pearse, but MacDonagh and Joseph Plunkett were poets, and all three merged their catholicism with intense, almost mystical nationalism. Others though – and Connolly is the best example – believed the spark might just catch fire throughout Ireland. This is not to suggest that when the time came Pearse and the romantics did not fight to win; or that Connolly had no doubts about the probable out-

The Recruiting Sergeant. *When Sergeant (later Major) Mick O'Leary VC and fellow wounded Irishmen arrived in London (left) on a recruitment drive, thousands turned out to greet them. In Dublin they were welcomed as national heroes. (The first VC of the war was won posthumously by another Irishman, Lt Maurice Dease, on 23 August 1914.)*

National Volunteers, *led by William O'Malley MP (right). They were that majority of Redmond's volunteers who supported his pro-British stance over the war. O'Malley appears rather large for his mount but his bulk does not obscure the emphatic message. Nationalists competed with Unionists in urging recruitment, less for their loyalty to the status quo than the promise of Home Rule and the vision of a new forged Irish nation. Easter 1916 was to change all that. The Home Rule politician and Economics Professor, Tom Kettle, who had joined up in 1914, saw this clearly: 'These men will go down in history as heroes and martyrs, and I will go down – if I go down at all – as a bloody British officer.' Kettle was killed on the Somme and his words proved prophetic. Until very recently independent Ireland ignored the massive southern Irish contribution to the Great War.*

come – as he marched out with his tiny band on that Easter Monday he quietly remarked to an unengaged colleague: 'we are going out to be slaughtered.'

Augustine Birrell, the Chief Secretary of Ireland, was a true Liberal in that he saw no need to suppress the various Volunteer forces, as they periodically assembled for their marches. Most Volunteers were under Redmond's pro-government command; as for MacNeill's lot, it was thought safer to have them under surveillance in the open. Sir Matthew Nathan, the Under-Secretary, and thus permanently in Dublin, echoed his superior. Dublin Castle had its informers within the Volunteers movement, and they were reporting no untoward intentions. Also the government had an inestimable weapon on its side in Room 40 of Naval Intelligence at Whitehall, where intercepted German radio messages were decoded, thanks to the seizure of some German code books very early in the war.

While the authorities remained unaware of the planned Easter rising, they did know about projected German assistance. Although Casement's attempts to raise an Irish brigade from Irish prisoners in German camps had failed hopelessly, the Germans decided to send a small ship, laden with arms and disguised as a Norwegian freighter, to Kerry in time for the Easter attempt. By now a supernumerary and thoroughly dejected, Casement arrived at the same time by German submarine, intending to stop the rising, or if that proved impossible, then participate and be killed. Room 40 knew all the details. The munitions ship was intercepted, Casement arrested – and in London and Dublin, Birrell and Nathan congratulated themselves on scotching any potential disturbance.

Meanwhile in Dublin, the Military Council, having learnt of imminent German aid, decided to tell Eoin MacNeill the good news and persuade him to call out the entire Irish

Sir Roger Casement *at his trial for treason in London (left). By 1916 he had come a long way from his upper class, County Antrim protestant background. Knighted for work exposing the horrors suffered by natives working on rubber plantations in the Congo and Amazon, he then became converted to Irish nationalism to the extent of trying (forlornly) to raise an Irish brigade from prisoners of war in Germany. In April 1916, fresh off a German submarine and trying to stop the rising because he knew expected German aid was not going to be forthcoming, he had been arrested. On 3 August he was hanged for treason, the implementation of the sentence aided by the government surreptitiously circulating his private diaries which catalogued homosexual activities. The debate still continues whether or not these were forgeries, though most historians accept they are genuine.*

The smell of treason *was almost more than these British Regulars could stomach during the rising. In defending the quays, they took up firing positions behind barrels filled with rotting fish heads.*

Volunteers. Then came confusing reports of Casement's capture, but MacNeill's countermanding orders to cancel any action were partly negated by the IRB Military Council which was now determined on a rising come what may. In the event few Irish Volunteers in the country were certain of their instructions, and of those in Dublin only the inner core were firm as to their intentions – to start a rising not on Easter Sunday, that was now impossible, but the next day, Easter Monday.

That Monday morning about 1,600 men marched through the Dublin streets and occupied certain buildings. Perhaps 200 of these belonged to Connolly's Citizen Army, while the rest were those Irish Volunteers in on the secret plans and loyal to the Military Council. Later claims would have meant the whole male population of Dublin were in action. 'Where were you in 1916?' became the patriot's taunt – to which the cynic's smart retort was 'under the bed like you my friend'. Another irreverent answer to the question was 'But I wasn't

born then.' 'Oh, excuses, excuses.'

Shortly after 12 noon, Patrick Pearse emerged on to the steps of the General Post Office and proclaimed the insurgents to be the provisional government of the Irish Republic. The declaration called upon the people of Ireland to support them in their fight to be sovereign and independent. It had been written by Pearse and Connolly (responsible, it is said, for the socialist clauses in the document though these are hard to discern) and signed by these two, plus Tom Clarke, Sean MacDermott, Eamon Ceannt, Thomas MacDonagh and Joseph Plunkett. They then settled down to await the British government's response.

Four areas had been seized south of the river: the third battalion occupied the streets around Boland's Bakery under the command of Eamon de Valera; the fourth battalion was in the South Dublin Union building under Eamon Ceannt; the second battalion around Jacob's biscuit factory under Thomas MacDonagh; and the Citizen Army around St Stephen's Green

Dublin's fair city. *Karl Marx said that 'the defensive is the death of every armed rising', fair comment on 1916. The travesty of a barricade (top left) was not intended to be fought from, but merely to slow the advance of troops. For much of the week, sections of the city burnt freely since the fire brigade were unable to operate (left and above right).*

under Michael Mallin. North of the river there were just two units: the first battalion at the Four Courts under Edward Daly, and Headquarters at the General Post Office and O'Connell Street under the command of Pearse and Connolly. Once in position the hope was that they could hang on, beating off attacks, while the country rose to their support. In certain ways the scheme resembled 19th-century urban risings, although the revolutionaries tended to stay within the houses and avoided constructing spectacular Parisian-style barricades.

Apart from the doomed nature of the enterprise (on Easter Monday the insurgents were outnumbered by 3 to1 and within two days, after troop reinforcements, by 20 to1) there was an important tactical weakness. Both Dublin Castle and Trinity College, which straddled the gap between the insurgents north and south of the river, were left untaken. Once the authorities reasserted themselves across this central link, they were free to pick off the areas one by one.

In their efforts to pour more troops into Dublin, the British

Business as usual *for Dubliners in the shadow of the burned out General Post Office in O'Connell Street (left), headquarters of the insurgents and where Pearse had read out the proclamation of the Republic. This photograph is taken from Nelson's Pillar, itself blown up in 1966 as one of the (unsanctioned) 50-year-commemorations of Easter 1916.*

Soldiers ever-present *(right) to ensure there was no more trouble, and to clear up. In the end most of the inhabitants of the city helped with this task.*

Army did make one expensive mistake. When recently arrived recruits from England – some of whom thought they were in France – came up against de Valera's men, they suffered 230 casualties at Mount Street bridge before the position was carried. Mostly the Army sensibly took its time and waited for artillery to pound the rebel strongholds north of the river. Connolly had assumed, rather desperately, that no capitalist power would destroy private property. There was little conventional street fighting, to the frustration of the insurgents who kept expecting frontal assaults. South of the river some areas were barely attacked. The Citizen Army, stationed at St Stephen's Green, occupied themselves at first by digging trenches, but were forced to retreat to the Royal College of Surgeons by a machine-gun post on the roof of the Shelburne Hotel. Thereafter they were bottled up for the rest of the week. The battalion at Jacob's biscuit factory also found itself with little to do.

Those insurgent battalions under attack all resisted with determination. Most of the shelling was concentrated on the headquarters at the Post Office and the rebels were literally burnt out of their shelters. One by one they fell to enemy fire. Connolly was wounded in the arm, and then the leg, but managed to keep issuing orders while on a stretcher. Michael O'Rahilly (who liked to style himself The O'Rahilly in the manner of Gaelic chiefs) had not been privy to the rising, and indeed had passed on MacNeill's countermand; but once the business started he had appeared and now was killed leading a charge against an army barricade.

The battle lasted for the whole week and, unlike modern IRA actions, it was fought according to the rules of war. The insurgents attempted to wear uniforms – the Volunteers in heather green, the Citizen Army dark green – and although there were not enough to go round it was a clear attempt to distinguish between combatant and civilian. Both sides respected white flags when flown and looked after wounded prisoners. Inevitably there were some dark moments. Enthusiastic snipers, not all in uniform, maddened the troops; some innocent civilians in North King Street paid for this later. The celebrated Dublin character and full-time radical, Francis Sheehy-Skeffington, became the victim of Captain Bowen-Colthurst. (In 1912, as a passionate suffragist, Sheehy had determined to heckle the Prime Minister at a Dublin meeting. Forewarned, the ushers kept a close look out for him, in his distinctive avant garde plus-fours – but they failed to stop a red bearded priest from entering. There suddenly rang out the shrill refrain, 'Votes for Wee-men', and Sheehy had scored again.) Bowen-Colthurst also shot out of hand a harmless boy, a couple of magazine editors and four other men before a fellow officer (reviled by others) insisted he be removed from his post. Ultimately Bowen-Colthurst was tried, declared insane, sent to Broadmoor for twenty months, and then released to emigrate to Canada.

By the Saturday Pearse and Connolly realised there was no point continuing. They signed an unconditional surrender which was carried round to the three other functioning units (the South Dublin Union had surrendered earlier in the week) and the rebels were marched away. According to official figures, 116 troops, 16 police, and 318 insurgents and civilians

were killed. A rough total of 2,500 were wounded.

Then followed retribution. Martial law was in force and General Sir John Maxwell, who had been put into command halfway through the rising, was free to decide the appropriate scale. Army thinking would demand some sentences of death – and many in Britain or serving in France would agree. The rebels had struck while Britain was engaged in a massive struggle against Germany. The peculiar situation in Ireland, however, meant this might not be the wisest course – and so it was to prove. Maxwell's actions, more than any other factor, were the transforming agent to make an unpopular rising into a national triumph. Ultimately Pearse, and his blood sacrifice, were the winners. (Maxwell's previous record, in fact, was not encouraging: after the battle of Omdurman in the Sudan in 1898, the wounded enemy had been despatched on the orders of Major Maxwell who said 'a dead fanatic is the only one to

extend any sympathy to.' This caused protests in Britain at the time.)

Public reaction to the Dublin rising is hard to gauge. But the majority of Dubliners at first appeared to be stunned by the outbreak; then as the devastation and battle mounted, they seem to have become censorious of, if not hostile to, the insurgents. Redmond and middle-class nationalists certainly condemned the rising in strong language. Reaction in the countryside appears to have been more mixed. Three and a half thousand people were quickly arrested and the majority interned in Britain. Most were released and back in Ireland by Christmas. If many had departed innocent and ignorant of the rising, they returned rather more politicised: the internment camp at Frongoch in north Wales became known as the Sinn Fein university. But the real damage was done by the Dublin courts-martial. Ninety prisoners were condemned to death;

throughout early May announcements were made most mornings that another little batch had been shot. Eventually 15 men were executed; the rest of the sentences were commuted.

Few people in Ireland or England, including the Prime Minister, knew the details or how many were going to be shot. Eventually Asquith, stirred by the Irish MP John Dillon's passionate speech, travelled to Dublin and the executions stopped. To General Maxwell, and many others in authority, nothing unjust had occurred. But what Dillon had called 'the policy of dribbling executions' created a growing horror and then sympathy. As further details emerged, the mood swung abruptly.

One of the last shot, James Connolly, was so badly wounded he had to be tied, slumped, to a chair, but as the rifles were levelled managed to raise himself upright. Without doubt the aftermath of Easter 1916 proved to be the major reason why Irish opinion moved from supporting the constitutional nationalists – Dillon's and Redmond's party – to the physical force men. And since the Fenians were a secret organisation, public backing now went to what was perceived, inaccurately, as their political front – Sinn Fein.

Of all the comments on the rising the most potent was Yeats' poem 'Easter 1916', which he wrote later that year but delayed publishing until 1920. A lesser Yeats poem, but more interesting in a political sense, was 'Sixteen Dead Men'. (Casement had been tried and executed in England to complete the numbers.)

O but we talked at large before
The sixteen men were shot,
But who can talk of give and take,
What should be and what not
While those dead men are loitering there
To stir the boiling pot?

Random searches *(left) by regular troops after it was all over. Almost the first casualties on the government's side had been inflicted, in fact, on some ancient reservists – the loyalist Dublin and Rathmines Volunteer Corps (below) distinguished by armbands carrying the initials GR (Georgius Rex) and known by Dubliners as the* *'Gorgeous Wrecks'. On Easter Monday they were returning from a route march with guns but no ammunition when they ran into the insurgents' third battalion: six men were killed before their inoffensive nature was realised. General Sir John Maxwell (carrying papers) inspects the survivors as they strain to attention.*

CHAPTER FOUR

INDEPENDENCE – AT
A PRICE

BEFORE 1914 SINN FEIN HELD NO SEATS IN Parliament, although the party had been in existence for nearly a decade and had contested one by-election. In the general election after the war in 1918 they achieved practically a clean sweep (minus the unionist north-east): 73 out of the 105 seats, at the expense of the old Irish parliamentary party which retained just 6. And the most important reason for this astonishing transference of political allegiance was the identification in people's minds of Sinn Fein with the glorious deeds of 1916. Fortunately for Arthur Griffith he had been arrested in the general clear out after the rising: a period of imprisonment at the hands of the British oppressor was fast becoming the necessary passport to a political career. Suddenly the whole nationalist process took an enormous step towards the physical force men and their ideal: the Republic as proclaimed from the steps of the GPO by Patrick Pearse.

This change was illustrated in a by-election in February 1917, when the father of one of those executed after Easter l916 was elected as Sinn Fein member of parliament – and then in accordance with abstentionist tactics refused to take his seat. Sinn Fein proceeded to win another six by-elections, one by Eamon de Valera (the only commandant of 1916 whose death sentence had been reprieved, possibly because of his American connections) and each time the little band of abstentionists grew.

The campaign was given further impetus by the death of Thomas Ashe, weakened by forcible feeding while on hunger strike for political status. Ashe had been the only Volunteer to conduct an effective operation at Ashbourne outside Dublin city in Easter 1916. At his funeral, superbly stage managed by the Sinn Fein–Volunteer combination, Michael Collins, a 26-year-old veteran of the GPO in 1916, stepped forward to give the oration. He provided a very different speech to the rhetorical tour de force delivered by Pearse at O'Donovan Rossa's graveside in 1915. This time there were only two sentences: 'Nothing additional remains to be said. The volley which we have just heard is the only speech which it is proper to make above the grave of a dead Fenian.'

The government could do little to save matters for the constitutionalists, preoccupied as it was with the conduct of the war in France, which reached a crisis with the German spring offensive of 1918. From this flowed the singleminded hunt for manpower, which in turn meant the decision to introduce conscription for Ireland.

Accounts rendered. *As if settling up the balance sheet for British rule in Ireland, a clerk examines a surviving ledger after the burning of James Gandon's imposing 18th-century Custom House by the IRA in May 1921. It and the Four Courts were major casualties from among Dublin's great heritage of Georgian architecture. Unfortunately they have been joined by a great many other distinguished buildings subsequently, though these have been victims of philistinism not violence.*

Hardly a ripple *seemed to disturb the surface of everyday life in the countryside during the Troubles. School children still assembled for their class photograph in Golden, County Tipperary (left), and the Rushbrooke ferry on the Lee continued forward and back (above). However, the first inci-dent in the war was rural, when Dan Breen, Sean Tracy and Seamus Robinson shot dead two policemen in the Soloheadbeg ambush in January 1919. Later this same group launched one of the many fruitless attempts to assassinate the viceroy, Lord French.* [PHOTOS: FR. BROWNE S. J.]

Ministers were aware of the hatred for this measure but hoped, rather desperately, that a renewed promise to implement Home Rule would sugar the pill. Instead there was condemnation from all sections of Irish opinion, except Ulster. Redmond's parliamentary party and the Church joined in, and were seen, inevitably, as dancing to Sinn Fein's tune. If this were not sufficient, the government then managed to give an added boost to Sinn Fein by arresting their leaders. This proved a godsend for the general election when several candidates were able to utilise the brilliant slogan of 'Vote him in to get him out'.

After the general election one cabinet minister, Walter Long, certainly saw things clearly: 'it is a fair and square fight between the Irish Government and Sinn Fein as to who is going to govern the country.' For Sinn Fein policy was dramatically simple: withdrawal from Westminster; establishment of a parliament in Dublin; the appointment of ministers to run the country. Britain was to be ignored, and for many months the authorities were not quite certain how to respond. In January 1919 Sinn Fein duly set up its own parliament, called the Assembly of Ireland or Dail Eireann. It confirmed de Valera as President (Griffith had withdrawn in his favour in 1917) and the commitment to a Republic. Instead of being impeded, its meetings at the Mansion House in Dublin were actually guarded by the police. It was not until the Dail started taking responsibility for the growing violence of the Volunteers that the government proscribed it and Sinn Fein in September 1919.

This reaction was just what the more extreme nationalists were looking for. Their strategy was to provoke the government into repressive policies, and then rely upon the innate liberalism of the British public, stiffened by world opinion, to recoil from using effective means to suppress the ensuing violence. The Volunteers now began calling themselves the Irish Republican Army. The IRB itself was falling out of favour. Many believed, as was hard to dispute, that its obsession with secrecy had harmed the effectiveness of the Easter rising, and pious types, such as de Valera, felt uneasy about the oath. Many simply dropped their membership without a qualm; one man said taking the IRB oath was like being inoculated – you forgot about it afterwards. Yet Michael Collins valued his own membership and used his position as president of the supreme council to advantage when it came to forging loyalties.

One war ended, another begun.
Men of the famous Irish Regiments march through Dublin for the August victory parade of 1919. Thousands turned out to watch, including these intrepid spectators on the roof of

Trinity College, the growing struggle for independence having, as yet, little impact on the general population, still prepared to sit under the Union Jack. That was all to change.
[PHOTO: JOSEPH CASHMAN]

An Auxiliary *engages a postman with the mail cart in a little light conversation (left). Other 'Auxies', distinctive in their Tam o' Shanter bonnets, desultorily watch proceedings. The Auxiliaries were further reinforcements for the police after the initial recruitment of the Black and Tans: they were paid more, largely kept their separate uniform (unlike the Tans who eventually received the full RIC rig) and were definitely more badly behaved.*

Fighting lasted from 1919 to the truce in July 1921. The style of warfare was that of a guerrilla struggle and hence quite different from Easter 1916. There was no open warfare; no fronts; no rival headquarters or strategic objectives to be stormed. The IRA did not wear uniforms. Their job was to make British administration impossible in Ireland and force their withdrawal. The campaign only gradually escalated in intensity. The first shooting, in January 1919 of two policemen guarding supplies of gelignite, set the tone for the early stages – raids for arms and attacks on the police. Then came attempts to destroy outposts of the RIC and police barracks themselves. In the first six months of 1920, for example, 16 occupied barracks were destroyed and 29 damaged; in addition the IRA burned over 400 abandoned posts. Forty-seven courthouses also went up in flames, a reminder that Sinn Fein was covering the country with their own alternative law courts. The armed services' response to these attacks was to round up members, and suspected members, of the IRA; this is turn led to the final phase of the war, when men left their homes and went on the run, many to form the celebrated flying columns. In the last year the war became mobile and large-scale ambushes were a feature.

Fighting was largely between the RIC and the IRA – demonstrated in the casualty figures after it was all over. Security services killed numbered 400 policemen and 160 soldiers. IRA and civilians killed amounted to 752. In spite of the British Army's involvement the official line was to brand the fighting as a disturbance by a small minority of 'gunmen' and thus worthy only of police attention. (In Ireland the police had always been an armed force.) Above all, the government felt the confrontation should not be dignified by the title of war, or anything which might suggest equality of the belligerents. Nationalists did regard it as a war, of course, by the army of an elected assembly against a foreign power. Many preferred the characteristic euphemism of The Troubles.

The Dublin Metropolitan Police, *initially unarmed, were easy targets, hence this sergeant's watchful eye along the street as he waits for the driver to produce some identification (right). It is doubtful how much regulars, such as the sergeant, were helped by the presence of the Auxiliaries.*

'Just doing my job'. *Soldiers in Dublin appear a little lost while engaged in keeping the crowds back during one of the numerous street searches (above). Many of the troops lived normal barrack life, as in the rest of the United Kingdom, and were somewhat caught in the middle between the IRA, and the RIC and its reinforcements of Tans and 'Auxies'.*

An IRA body *is loaded into an ambulance (above) after the action to retake the Custom House in May 1921.*

The Big Fellow. *Negotiating the treaty in London, late 1921, Michael Collins allows himself to be caught in an unusual pose, smiling full face to the camera (left); during the Troubles he tried to avoid being photographed too clearly. De Valera, Collins' future opponent, takes the salute (right) of the IRA's western divsion at Six Mile Bridge, County Clare; also watching, beyond the platform, a volunteer holds one of the new Thompson sub-machine-guns, smuggled in from America from May 1921.*

In many aspects the conflict was conducted at a hesitant, almost courteous level. The Anglo-Irish writer, Hubert Butler, tells of two men arriving at the family house to demand material support for the IRA. Butler, then an undergraduate at Oxford, was fascinated to meet a flesh-and-blood Republican and longed to engage him in political discussion; but Butler's mother had other concerns. "'I know who you are", she said to one of them. "You're Jim Connell. Take your cigarette out of your mouth when you're talking to me." He took it out and I began to scold my mother for interrupting what might have been a revealing conversation … My mother answered me sharply and we started an angry argument. The two men looked at each other in embarrassment and slunk politely away.'

By 1920 the government realised that, if the police were to continue holding the front line, then reinforcements were necessary. Recruitment had fallen off (understandably) in Ireland and so new men were enlisted in England from amongst ex-servicemen. First arrivals in Ireland found a lack of police uniforms and so were forced to wear a hybrid assembly of khaki coats and bottle-green RIC trousers and caps. Wits christened them the Black and Tans after a Tipperary hunt (the Scarteen), so named for the colouring of its hounds. Further police reinforcements came later in 1920 with the arrival of the Auxiliary Division. Again these were English veterans, but this time ex-officers. They were given a special uniform – dark blue with glengarry caps – and paid double the rate of normal RIC recruits.

These two groups lacked police experience or training and soon began to make a reputation for themselves for brutal conduct. Their commanders hardly inspired respect. The Auxiliaries, popularly known as the Auxies, were generally the least disciplined. Their leader was an ex-UVF officer (hardly a neutral choice one might have thought), Brigadier Crozier, who distinguished himself first by encouraging Auxiliary thuggery and then by resigning from what he described as a drunken and insubordinate body of men – a sensational exit. The overall commander of the RIC was General Tudor, an officer with no previous police experience and an excitable temperament. It is true that the British Army commander in Ireland, General Macready, was most competent and judicious. He had been one of the few senior officers the Liberal government could trust over the Ulster crisis in 1914 and he also had much police experience. He harboured no warm feelings for Ireland itself, once writing to a new Chief Secretary with these comforting words: 'I cannot say I envy you for I loathe the country you are going to and its people with a depth deeper than the sea and more violent than that which I feel against the Boche.' Nevertheless Macready probably did as well as circum-

stances allowed in Ireland, although his contempt for these RIC reinforcements meant co-operation between the Army and Police was never the best. In February 1921 he complained that the Auxiliaries 'treat the martial law areas as a special game preserve for their amusement'. The Auxies liked to make their presence felt by roaring up and down the countryside, often at night, in their big Crossley tenders.

The difficulty for the security forces was coping with a guerrilla campaign. Where was the enemy? Who indeed was the enemy? The number of active IRA men was in fact fairly small, perhaps no more than 3,000 at any one time. Yet operatives moved easily from combatant to civilian status and back again; full strength might have been four times that number. Opposing them were about 14,000 police, including the English reinforcements, and 25,000 troops. But the IRA enjoyed that crucial advantage any successful guerrilla force

needs: backing from the local population. Whether in Napoleonic Spain, French Algeria, or Vietnam in the 1960s, if the people broadly supported fighters in the field then the battle could be won.

And this is the story of the Anglo-Irish war. Of course the dividing lines were never that neatly drawn. There were loyalists in the south who would abet the security forces, and many neutral people with strong views for neither side. Terrorism was applied by the IRA to civilians, ranging from damaging property to the shooting of 'spies and informers'. But unlike their opponents, the IRA were working with the grain: most of the population (always excepting the north-east) was genuinely anti-British. While not agreeing with the methods, many felt an admiration for the boys in the field. Some in significant places shared the IRA's view that they were soldiers fighting with the only means at their disposal. 'I shot a man, Father', said one

The Prime Minister, *David Lloyd George, and Sir Hamar Greenwood inspecting Auxiliaries in the quadrangle of the Foreign Office (right). A total of 1,800 of these ex-Army officers were recruited to serve as officer cadets of the RIC, from July 1920 to the end of 1921. One of their successful actions was the capturing of 120 IRA volunteers at the burning of the Custom House.*

gunman at confession. 'Did you think you were doing right?', the priest asked. When assured that he did, the priest said, 'carry on with the good work' and gave him absolution. Previous physical force movements, such as the Fenians in the 19th century, had been riddled by informers and the IRA was determined, by cultural pressure and terrorism when necessary, to ensure no weaknesses now. Such a grip on the community meant their intelligence system, under the control of Michael Collins, was more effective than the Crown's, at least until the last six months of the war.

Undeniably Collins was the central figure behind the IRA's campaign. He has been described, not too fancifully, as the founder of modern guerrilla warfare, or urban terrorism; and his organisational ability, decisive action, nerve and sheer charisma made him an inspirational figure for the Irish and an enemy to be respected by the British. 'The tenacity of the IRA is extraordinary', exclaimed the Cabinet Secretary, Tom Jones, to Bonar Law in April 1921. 'Where was Michael Collins during the Great War? He would have been worth a dozen brass-hats.' Collins came from a small but self-confident farming household in County Cork. Once, when he broke into Dublin Castle to examine police files, he was amused to find his own file began 'He comes from a brainy Cork family'. At 16, he moved to a clerical job in London, educating himself further in the evenings. Already a member of the IRB for some years, he returned to Ireland in 1915 and fought in the Easter rising the next year. In the Anglo-Irish war, the Big Fellow, as he was known by his followers, created a network of agents, some even from within Dublin Castle. This enabled him to use his special hit team, known as the Squad, on specific assassination missions. The most spectacular of these occurred very early on the morning of 21 November 1920, when the Squad shot dead 12 British officers, members and co-ordinators of the 'Cairo' gang, the elite of government intelligence. Later that

A shifty Black and Tan *reloads his .45 revolver flamboyantly (left), while a Tommy leans forward as if he has never before seen such an exotic sight. Behind, arrested suspects stand with their hands on their heads.*

day, some Auxiliaries appeared at Croke Park, where a big Gaelic football match was being played, and with unconscious symmetry also killed 12 people by shooting into the stadium. Known as Bloody Sunday, this double episode has been treated with panache by Neil Jordan in his recent film (1997) *Michael Collins*. However, some rough factual edges had to be smoothed for visual effect. Perhaps two of the officers shot were not secret service agents (though the British counter-claim at the time that they were all ordinary regimental officers is nonsense) and Jordan's cinematic coup of the police's armoured car swivelling like a Dalek and spitting out streams of bullets is invention. No armoured car was present and it is doubtful if machine-guns were used – otherwise casualties must surely have been higher. Nevertheless the afternoon was an astonishing breakdown of discipline and exploited to the full by republican propaganda.

Bodies *of the assassinated intelligence agents were taken on gun-carriages through Kingstown (now Dun Laoghaire) (below) flanked by mourning troops, their arms reversed, over the Irish Sea to a state funeral in London.*

Collins himself led a charmed life, cycling around Dublin quite openly despite the price on his head. He was always careful to look like a respectable businessman on the principle that at British checkpoints the troops could not imagine terrorists dressed in neat grey suits. Another principle he gleaned from a remark made by one of the anarchists in G. K. Chesterton's *The Man who was Thursday*: 'If you don't seem to be hiding, nobody hunts you out.' Several times, though, he had to bluff his way past security checks. He took care to avoid being photographed full face and in a number of group photographs – Sinn Fein business or social occasions such as weddings – he would try and hide behind others or lower his head.

The same month as Bloody Sunday Tom Barry's west Cork flying column scored a dramatic success when they ambushed and wiped out an Auxiliary patrol of 16 men at Kilmichael. If the government was going to have a chance of winning the war, new methods would have to be applied. The military had been pressing for martial law for some time, and now at last they got it. To the fury of Macready, however, only eight counties (Munster province plus Kilkenny and Wexford) fell under this jurisdiction. 'I fully realise the difficulty this partial application of martial law means', Macready wrote to his deputy, 'but the frocks [the Generals' superbly contemptuous nickname for politicians] were firm, not to impose it all over.' To exempt major ports, and especially Dublin, was illogical.

The Cairo Gang *(above) were government intelligence agents so called because of their Middle Eastern experience. Their boss was that 'most amazing original' Colonel Ormonde Winter, never without his monocle and black cigarette holder, described by a senior official as resembling 'a wicked little white snake, clever as paint, probably entirely non-moral'. Twelve members of the Gang and other British intelligence officers were shot dead by Collins' men one Sunday morning in November 1920.*

An unwelcome visit *(left). Auxies dismount from their Crossley tenders prior to a search in County Tipperary; this is a scene of calm but the Auxies regularly fired in the air on their travels and lobbed thunderflashes into crowds, terrifying the innocent and embarrassing the authorities. The superstructures covered in chicken wire were to deflect any hand grenades that the IRA might try and throw into the trucks.*

Balbriggan, north of Dublin *(right), after the Tans had taken reprisals for a murdered policeman: a hosiery factory, four pubs and 49 other houses were burnt, and two locals killed.*

The government was never that comfortable about the introduction of martial law, however, and full support was missing.

Surprisingly, ministers were sometimes more enthusiastic about another tactic which appears far less legal and orderly – 'official' reprisals. Unofficial reprisals had been exacted for some time, usually by the Tans and Auxies, probably the most spectacular of which was the burning of Cork city centre around St Patrick Street in December 1920. Now the process became systematised, and property would be burnt in reprisal for ambushes and other outrages. The trouble with this was that the loss often fell on landlords, and in any case the IRA immediately commenced counter reprisals by burning Anglo-Irish mansions – these great houses made easy targets, isolated throughout the countryside. One local IRA leader summed up the policy when he woke Lord Bandon while sprinkling petrol around his rooms at night: 'You burned my castle last week. Now I'll burn yours.' After five months the government dropped the practice.

Yet it continued to countenance summary punishments of individuals – reprisal murders. It was believed that the violence was being enacted by small bodies of unrepresentative gunmen; surgically remove these individuals and all would be well. It is clear that elements in cabinet – certainly the Prime Minister, Churchill and Greenwood – were prepared to endorse 'gunning': letting the security forces shoot known gunmen. But to

the disgust of the Army, the politicians refused to make these shootings an official policy; they preferred to be able to disclaim responsibility if challenged. Such cynicism shook even the rabidly Unionist General Wilson at the War Office, who wrote in his diary: 'Tudor made it very clear that the police and the Black and Tans and the 100 Intell: officers are all carrying out reprisal murders … At Balbriggan, Thurles and Galway yesterday the local police marked down certain SF's as in their opinion the actual murderers or instigators and then coolly went and shot them without question or trial. Winston saw very little harm in this but it horrifies me.'

So the viciousness mounted on both sides. Dark deeds were reported from within Dublin Castle and various barracks (here Jordan's film is broadly persuasive), and a number of IRA men were reported as 'shot while trying to escape'. Men in high office also suffered. The Lord Mayor of Cork, Terence MacSwiney, died after 74 days on hunger strike for political status; his successor, Thomas MacCurtain, was shot in his house (the coroner bringing a verdict of guilty against Lloyd George, the Home Secretary and the local RIC who had, in fact, done the deed; the man responsible, District Inspector Swanzy, was sent north for protection, but the IRA caught up with him in the end). The Lord Mayor of Limerick was also shot out of hand by security forces. Informers continued to be 'executed' by the IRA, on one occasion a 70-year-old lady who

had warned the Army of an impending ambush. Several times the IRA threatened to shoot captured English officers to try and save their fellows awaiting execution in British gaols – and in some areas carried out the threat. Ernie O'Malley's force shot three English officers in reprisal near Clonmel. As they marched the men through the fields in the early morning dew, one of the victims remarked conversationally, 'stiff banks those for hunting'. 'There's not much hunting now', said O'Malley, hating himself and his duty. Frank O'Connor's fine short story, 'Guests of the Nation', plays upon the same tragic theme.

A splendid example of the Auxies in full cry occurred in April 1921 when they raided an hotel in County Limerick in the hope of capturing suspects. The plan was for 14 men in plain clothes to enter the hotel bar to determine targets, while 21 others surrounded the hotel. As they approached the hotel a number of men were seen running across the fields, and in their excitement the original plan was forgotten. The plain-clothed Auxiliaries rushed into the bar shouting 'Hands up!' Unfortunately there were three off-duty RIC men drinking there, who quite naturally assumed the intruders to be IRA. The two parties blazed away at each other, the men at the bar succeeding in driving out their perceived attackers. Eventually

A Tan raid on Liberty Hall, the headquarters of the Irish Trade Union Congress in Dublin, on 25 November 1920, a few days after Bloody Sunday. Finding nothing, the police decided to depart with some cultural loot – musical instruments belonging to the Union's band.

unsavoury information and rumours kept finding their way to the British press. Even government sympathisers found the official line difficult to swallow. 'There is no such thing as reprisals, but they have done a great deal of good' was Lord Hugh Cecil's apt summary of Greenwood's explanations.

Although Lloyd George refused to admit the revolt was a war, he had not come up with any political initiatives for Ireland. The British government was involved with the settlement of post-war Europe in 1919, admittedly, but the cabinet's minds were slow to turn towards Ireland even after the various European treaties had been signed. Eventually, in December 1920, it applied what had broadly been agreed on in the summer of 1914. The only trouble was that events had moved on since then, especially in the south of Ireland.

The Government of Ireland Act (1920) partitioned the island and gave both areas Home Rule. In effect this meant separate parliaments for Dublin and Belfast, each with powers of self-government. Overarching and linking these parliaments was the Council of Ireland to provide some sort of Irish unity – but this remained a shadowy concept, depending on agreement between the two parliaments. Because no nationalists were consulted over the boundary, this line favoured the unionists. Interestingly the cabinet had proposed the whole of Ulster, nine counties, for exclusion; though a minority preferred local plebiscites in the fashion established by US President Woodrow Wilson to secure a division of post-war Europe, based on self-determination. If all nine counties had been excluded this would have meant a unit almost equally divided between protestants and catholics, and hence less able to be controlled by the unionists. These implacable men – with their allies in cabinet, such as Carson and Curzon – instead insisted, and got, the six north-eastern counties. Although this unit included catholic majorities in Tyrone and Fermanagh, it was felt they could be overawed. It was a casual way to construct a border and one which could hardly be expected to last without protest.

Long sought by the South, Home Rule was now insufficient after the glories of 1916 and electoral triumphs of Sinn Fein. As so often in the relationship between Britain and Ireland, it was a matter of too little and too late. But the Sinn Fein alternative government gratefully used the mechanism for elections to this unwanted parliament to prove, once again, their complete dominance in the south. They won every single seat in May 1921, apart from the unnatural unionist stronghold of Dublin University. The political message – that nationalist Ireland spoke with one voice and that voice demanded independence – was unequivocal.

Nevertheless the war continued. It is hard to determine who was getting the upper hand. Army intelligence had been reorganised and had been achieving some successes in discovering arms dumps. It also introduced what has been described as the only true counter-guerrilla tactic during the conflict: the employment of mobile, self-contained foot patrols, dropped

the uniformed Auxiliaries arrived, and the RIC men within the hotel realised their mistake. They ran out to surrender along with the landlord, but the Auxies continued to fire, killing the landlord and wounding one of the RIC. It ended with three dead and many wounded. According to an eminent hotel guest, brother of Lord Parmoor, the Auxies then stormed around the hotel 'like demented Red Indians'. The government's reaction to this imbroglio was impassively to deny any indiscipline or untoward action; Hamar Greenwood, the Home Secretary, became a master at baldfaced denials interspersed with defence on the grounds of necessary action. Yet

The American card *was used by both nationalists and unionists. American and Canadian Orangemen (left) attend a 12th of July parade in Belfast in 1920. American flags are sold in Dublin (right) during the Truce in late 1921; (below) the tall, sleek figure of de Valera and Archbishop Hayes on St Patrick's Day in New York, 1919.*

into the countryside and operating in random directions. Later the British in Malaya and the Americans in Vietnam would adopt similar methods. There is some evidence that this new strategy was producing results. During the subsequent treaty negotiations Michael Collins admitted to one of the British delegation that Irish resistance, at the current intensity, could not have continued for more than three weeks.

Yet the IRA were still in business. Flying columns were flaunting themselves with even greater impunity; the countryside was behind them more than ever; financially Sinn Fein was flush from de Valera's fund-raising campaign in America in 1919–20. And Collins had now got his hands on the brand new Thompson sub-machine-guns and a number were in use by June 1921, enabling later patriots to bellow ballads about 'the rattle of the Thompson gun'.

What swung the balance was public opinion. In Ireland this was simply polarised; in the world it was mixed; but in England liberal public opinion – that great force, often myopic when it came to Ireland – at last roused itself. Stories about police excesses had been reaching the press, despite official disclaimers; emotional nationalism, best seen in Yeats' poems, began to work its magic; republican propaganda proved

increasingly adept at exploiting the story of a gallant nation and heavy booted oppressors. Above all, there was the awkward fact that the electorate had decided three times (twice in general elections, once at local level) to reject hesitant British offers of partial self-government and press for independence. The British spirit prided itself on responding to the cry for freedom – even, it was now reluctantly admitting, to a demand for freedom from Britain. It was this mood which forced Lloyd George to abandon plans to defeat the rebels and offer a truce in order to negotiate directly with Sinn Fein. He also dropped conditions which would have prevented any meeting: the demand that the IRA surrender its arms and a refusal to allow Collins and other prominent 'gunmen' to form part of the Irish negotiating team. The actual catalyst for the government's demarche was probably the favourable public response, in England and Ireland, to King George V's plea for reconciliation when opening the northern parliament in June. The truce followed at noon on 11 July 1921. Just before it came into operation the local IRA in Cork killed an old RIC sergeant as he dug his garden – a reminder that the boys were undefeated and still in business.

Neither side won the war in a military sense. There is no

George V, *ready to open the Parliament in Northern Ireland after the Government of Ireland Act (1920) had partitioned the island, here (above) inspects the RIC, shortly to become the Royal Ulster Constabulary. The King's speech in June 1921, pleading for reconciliation, was a factor in preparing the way for the Truce between the IRA and the British the following month.*

Cheers all round *from the crowd outside the Mansion House in Dublin as delegates arrive for a conference on 8 July 1921 to discuss the terms of a truce (right). General Macready and the southern Unionists' leader, Lord Midleton, were surprised to be cheered as loudly as their opponents. The Truce went into effect at noon on Monday 11 July.*

Under Nelson's Column *in London's Trafalgar Square (above) Irish tricolour flags were held aloft without causing public protest, proof that by late 1921 the British people were beginning to accept the idea of an Irish nation.*

A young patriot sings *to the crowd outside Dublin's Mansion House as the final details of the Truce were being hammered out in July 1921.*

doubt that the British could have poured in resources to restore order, even if it had to be under martial law. The police by themselves – even with, or despite, the Black and Tan reinforcements – could not have done this; but the Army could. Reliance on the military option alone required the government's wholehearted backing, which in turn needed the full support of British public opinion, and that was beginning to disappear by 1922. The IRA's success came from the fact that it kept on going until the British government was forced to the negotiating table. In political terms the Irish were the victors.

Trying to sell the Treaty.
Bareheaded in the rain amidst a sea of hats, Michael Collins attempts to persuade Dubliners of the virtues of the Anglo-Irish Treaty in March 1922. Symbolically enough, the platform is set up in front of the portico of the Bank of Ireland, that had been the Irish Parliament in the 18th century. The Treaty provided for effective, but not complete, independence for southern Ireland: it also confirmed partition, with the six north-eastern counties remaining part of Britain.

CHAPTER FIVE

SETTLEMENTS AND COMPROMISE

T HE TRUCE WAS POPULAR IN IRELAND. MAKING HIS way to a meeting with the Irish leaders a few days before the declaration, General Macready was surprised to find himself cheered by the Dublin crowd. The common mood seemed to be that the physical force men had done their bit, and that now was the time for peace and an agreed settlement. Despite this easy optimism any compromise was going to be difficult. The British clearly would have to advance from their pre-war Home Rule offer, but were unlikely to allow full independence. The Irish had been fighting for a republic which it was assumed meant not only complete sovereignty but withdrawal from the Empire. Something would have to give.

The President of the Irish Republic, as yet unrecognised by Britain, was Eamon de Valera. Over the summer he met several times with Lloyd George, but neither man made much progress. Lloyd George complained that arguing with de Valera was like trying to pick up mercury with a fork; to which Dev is supposed to have replied, 'why doesn't he use a spoon?' Nevertheless after some weeks the Irish did agree to a formal conference with the British government, in Lloyd George's careful phrases, 'with a view to ascertaining how the association of Ireland with the community of nations known as the British Empire can best be reconciled with Irish national aspirations.'

The Irish delegation consisted of Arthur Griffith and Michael Collins, the two heavyweights; and E. J. Duggan, Robert Barton and George Gavan Duffy. De Valera was noticeably absent, his reason being to avoid damaging the dignity of the Presidency and that in any case he had already tried his best with Lloyd George; others might be more successful. Another explanation put forward by unkind people is that de Valera knew that a compromise was inevitable and that he was not going to be the one to sacrifice the Republic.

The senior of the three secretaries with the Irish delegation was Erskine Childers, a complex piece of work and a marvellous example of what has been designated the Marginal Men – that is English people who fall in love with a romantic, revolutionary ideal of Ireland. Childers' background was thoroughly upper-middle-class patriotic English: educated at Haileybury and Cambridge, he was a Boer War veteran and defender of England's security through his thriller *The Riddle of the Sands* (1903), one of the first books to warn of the German threat. Then some time before 1914 Childers took on the mantle of an Irish nationalist – perhaps influenced by his cousin Robert

Lord Dunsany's footmen *(above) still served drinks at a meet of the Meath Hunt in 1923. Lord Dunsany, man of letters and man of action, had been caught up in the Easter 1916 rising: he received a bullet through his cheek and was captured by the rebels, but got on so well with them that he gave one of them his British Army Sam Browne belt for a souvenir, which later ended up on Collins' body while it was lying in state.*

A fond farewell. *The Malahides and Dunsany might be staying on, but it was time to go for the constable guarding Viceregal Lodge (right). Mr Taylor, the Chief Steward, shakes him by the hand in December 1922.*

Lord and Lady Talbot de Malahide, *with Mrs Ryan (on the right) and 'two-and-a-half couple' of Irish wolfhounds, calmly view the society snapper taking their photograph in the mid 1920s. The family had arrived in Ireland with the Normans in the 12th century, and the Troubles of 1916–22 were just*

another phase in their long history. It was to take death duties, on the demise of the 7th Baron in 1973, to force the selling of their castle, which had been in continuous occupation by the Talbots since the medieval period. Around the date of this photograph, one of this century's greatest literary caches was discovered at Malahide: the papers of James Boswell, the biographer of Samuel Johnson. They eventually went to Yale University, having come from Scotland to Ireland in the first place on the marriage of a Boswell heiress to a Talbot.

Gaelic sports *enjoyed a resurgence, as the Free State came into being. One of the main athletic events was the 1924 Tailkeann games in Dublin's Croke Park, but all over the countryside there was much running and leaping, as at the Gaelic games (left) at Ballydavid, County Kerry. Gradually, though, the primacy of athletics declined as the emphasis was put on Gaelic football and hurling by the GAA.*
[PHOTO: FR. BROWNE S. J.]

The Senegalese boxer *Louis Phail (above), known as 'Battlin' Siki', in Dublin for a 1923 prize fight. Here a Dublin boy gets his chance to size up the light-heavyweight world champion, but Phail's title was lost in the fight to the Clareman, Mike McTaigue, who kept it until 1925. The Irish excelled at boxing. Irish Americans John L. Sullivan and James J. Corbett were world famous and world champions at the turn of the century.*

Barton and the memories of vacations in Barton's Wicklow home – and played a daring part in gunrunning for the Irish Volunteers. Yet once war broke out he rediscovered his imperial sympathies, being awarded a DSC while in the Royal Navy Air Service. It was back to fighting for Ireland after 1918, and an ever stronger conversion to the Holy Grail of the Republic. As we shall see, Childers took a rigid line over the defence of republican status; to a lesser extent so did the other two English public school educated men on the Irish delegation –

Barton (Rugby) and Duffy (Stonyhurst). Could it be that these English-sounding gentlemen were so anxious to establish their Irish credentials and avoid accusations of backsliding that they proved more implacable than the indubitably Irish Griffith and Collins?

Public school or not, the British imagined they would have little trouble outmanoeuvring the Irish team. The civil service in London produced an impertinent document which, after providing thumb-nail sketches of each delegate, concluded: the delegates 'will be nervous and ill at ease. They have never been in conference with men of experience before. They are leaders in Dail Eireann, which is a very nondescript assembly ... they may be a bit rude and extravagant in speech.' In the event the colonial hicks did not do badly. Collins in particular got the measure of his opponents; he too provided secret character sketches, and managed to skewer LG: 'Trusts that his fatherly air and benevolence will overcome all obstacles – craft again. "Now Michael ..." he says; or "Now Mick ..."... Would sell his nearest and dearest for political prestige.' Collins thought Greenwood loathsome, but was respectful of Churchill and positively admired Lord Birkenhead (F. E. Smith that was, and now more flexible than in his giddy days as a supporter of Ulster extremism pre 1914).

The issue was, how much independence should Ireland receive – what was to be its status? And what was to be its size? It might be surprising today, in view of Ulster's woes since l968, to discover that the second question, that of the North, did not preoccupy the conference. In fact the partition of Ireland in 1920 really allowed these treaty negotiations to go ahead the next year – because the unionist card had been removed. With the Ulster trump still in the pack there would have been an impasse straightaway. Of course, unionists in the south and nationalists in the north had to be sacrificed, but by accepting, if only temporarily, the division of Ireland, the Irish delegation showed their realism. Lloyd George helped them to this decision by offering a Boundary Commission which, it was strongly hinted, would prune nationalist Tyrone, Fermanagh, south Armagh and Derry, leading to an unviable statelet and eventual reunification. (At the same time the Prime Minister secretly guaranteed to Ulster unionists that the border would remain unchanged.)

The main question circled around the status of the new Ireland. In the end it had to be a compromise. The British agreed to concede dominion status, as enjoyed by Canada and the white Empire ex-Commonwealth as it was known. That meant the Head of State remained the King with his representative in Dublin (the Governor-General); various office holders, including parliamentarians, would have to take an oath of loyalty to the Crown. Ireland would still be part of the Empire, and hence subject to its collective pressure – whatever that might be. Various ports in the south would remain British territory for reasons of imperial security. On the other hand the Irish would gain complete independence in domestic matters, de facto independence in foreign affairs; and – or so the Irish delegation, especially Collins, argued when back in Dublin – in practice freedom to obtain eventual sovereignty. 'You can't create a Republic overnight', said Collins. Why worry about

The Welsh Wizard, *Lloyd George (far left) with two of his negotiating team for the Anglo-Irish Treaty, Lord Birkenhead and Winston Churchill, outside Number Ten. Collins was most impressed by Birkenhead: 'If all the British delegation had his capacity for clear thinking ... things would be much easier. Lawyer, but with a great difference ... a good man.'*

Erskine Childers *(right) led the secretaries to the Irish delegation. He was fated to be one of the first republicans executed by the new Irish government in the Civil War. To his right is his namesake and eldest son who was to become President of the Republic of Ireland in the 1970s.*

the exact form of words?

But back home some people did concern themselves about the sacrifice of the Republic – and the sacrifice of those who had died on its behalf, from the declaration in 1916 to the truce of 1921. And Collins knew this too: in another letter during the negotiations he admitted, 'if we accept at all it will be inferred as a gross betrayal'. His line, however, was to argue that the treaty, though insufficient in itself, could be a stepping stone to complete independence.

Since Collins has been proved right (with subsequent stones in 1933, 1937 and 1949), there has been a tendency to endorse his and Griffith's position. There is also natural sympathy for men who eschew the extremes and accept the middle ground. It might be asked, however, why Britain did not exert itself to grant the Irish what they wanted in 1921, instead of grudgingly permitting limited sovereignty and insisting on the oath. By refusing republican status in 1921, the British set the scene for a most bloody civil war in Ireland between republican diehards and compromisers. Moreover, a plan for a republic, but in association with the Commonwealth, existed courtesy of de Valera, actually anticipating India's status in 1947. The Long Fellow, as de Valera sometimes was known (after his height of course but, with its faint suggestion of deviousness, a more wary sobriquet than Collins' the Big Fellow) has taken the blame in the history books, but perhaps the real indictment should be levelled at Lloyd George and his team, who demonstrated a lack of political courage (glancing over their shoulders at the unionist vote) and, most importantly, a failure of the imagination.

Right up to the signing of the treaty on 6 December 1921, matters hung in the balance. Nobody on the Irish side was happy with the abandonment of the republic and the necessity of the oath; and until that last day only Griffith was prepared to sign. Then the Welsh Wizard produced his theatricals. Waving two letters in their faces, Lloyd George solemnly intoned that both were to Sir James Craig, the Ulster unionist leader in Belfast. One was to say that Sinn Fein had accepted the terms of the treaty, the other to say they had not. 'If I send this letter it is war – and war within three days.' Was it bluff? Impossible to tell. In the short term the British could do what they wanted; but that also would have involved returning to square one.

After much agonised deliberation, the Irish delegation unanimously signed in the early hours of the morning. Lloyd George and Birkenhead both stressed to Collins the possible cost to themselves. Collins remained unimpressed with the former. ' "Got my political life at stake", [Lloyd George had confided to him some weeks earlier]. I didn't answer him. My life – not only political – is at stake.' And in another letter sent to the same friend on the day after the signing Collins wrote: 'Think – what have I got for Ireland? Something which she has wanted these past seven hundred years. Will anyone be satisfied at the bargain? Will anyone? I tell you this – early this

morning I signed my death warrant.' In this prediction, as in so much else, Michael Collins was dead right.

The Anglo-Irish treaty now had to be endorsed by the Dail. A passionate debate commenced at the end of the year and into January 1922. The accusation against the Irish signatories was that they had exceeded their powers, being delegates rather than plenipotentiaries, and had come home with a treaty which still gave authority to the King of Great Britain. It was the simple matter of the oath which most split the assembly. Throughout the debate, which ran from 14 December to 7 January with a break for Christmas, the North was hardly mentioned – an illustration of how embarrassing that region was for

An unsporting shot. *Field Marshal Sir Henry Wilson was a sitting duck when gunned down by the IRB on a London street. 'At heart a politician rather than a soldier', he came from among the Anglo-Irish gentry of County Longford. Deeply involved in the 1914 Curragh incident, he was an implacable enemy of Irish nationalism and after his resignation from the Army became a Unionist MP and great supporter of the B Specials' activities in the North. In a statement at their trial his two assassins (shortly after their capture, right) claimed him as 'the man behind the Orange Order ... he raised and organised a body known as the Ulster Special Constables who are the principal agents in his campaign of terrorism.'*

nationalists advocating the principle of self-determination. Before the debate the seven-man cabinet had split, with Griffith, Collins, Cosgrave and Barton in favour; the President, de Valera, Brugha and Stack against. The vote in the Dail was similarly close – 64 to 57 in approval of the Treaty articles. De Valera resigned and Griffith took his place.

A General Election was set for June, to establish the country's verdict, but the pro and anti Treaty camps were already moving further apart; the key area became control over the armed forces. Collins was near despair at the division within the revolutionary movement and came close to arranging a strange pact with de Valera, to provide a set number of seats at the forthcoming election. In these hectic post-treaty months Collins did go beyond legal means in his efforts to keep the republicans on board; an extreme example was his order for the assassination of General Sir Henry Wilson, shot on the steps of his London house in June 1922. Neither Griffith nor the British government realised Collins was responsible; his immediate motive appears to have been that Wilson was behind the attacks on catholics in the North. Yet Wilson's constant machinations on behalf of unionism, from the Curragh incident onwards, had been enough to damn him in nationalist eyes. His comment on the Treaty was a classic last hurrumph: 'The agreement is a complete surrender. 1. A farcical oath of allegiance. 2.

Playing at soldiers *in the phoney war during the spring of 1922. Children (above) practise drilling outside the Four Courts, the country's central law courts, seized* *and sandbagged by anti-Treaty forces on 14 April; more children (right) prepare to ambush the postman.*

Republicans lower the tricolour *prior to evacuating Dublin's Masonic Hall as the two sides in the Civil War move to open hostility.*

Withdrawal of our troops. 3. A rebel army, etc., etc. The British Empire is doomed.' The assassins were two ex-servicemen, one with a wooden leg after Ypres; clearly this hampered their getaway and they were captured and later hanged.

In the June election the country voted in favour of the Treaty by nearly 2 to 1. But significantly most votes were cast for Labour and Independent candidates; not only a protest vote at both political camps but an indication of rising interest in socialism. Limerick, of all places, had proclaimed a short-lived Soviet in 1919; the red flag was flown from some Tipperary creameries in 1922, and disturbances were rife throughout that year. However, the Provisional Government, soon to become the Irish Free State, ignored such left-wing (and in fact traditional agrarian) rumblings, and now felt they could start effective governing, backed by a mandate from the country. The IRA had continued to split, with anti-treaty commanders and troops simply refusing to obey orders from the Provisional Government, and those who supported the treaty becoming the Free State army. Their opponents were dubbed the Irregulars or more accurately known simply as republicans. Collins' influence was vital in keeping top men with the Free State. (General Macready, morosely observing events, imagined that no one would follow Griffith since the South was so strongly republican.) The army chief, Richard Mulcahy, was loyal to the provisional government, as was another very young General, Emmet Dalton, perhaps the most interesting officer engaged in the Civil War. Dalton had fought in the Great War, being made a major in his early twenties and winning the MC; he then became Collins' right-hand man and leading strategist of the Munster campaign in the Civil War; afterwards he moved to England and emerged as a film producer. On the opposite side were heroes old and young such as Liam Lynch, Rory O'Connor and the dashing Tom Barry from west Cork. De Valera joined the anti-treaty forces but in a non-military capacity. Both Free State and Irregular officers were fond of promoting themselves to the rank of general. The first Governor-General of the Irish Free State, Timothy Healy, was once asked by a lady guest at a reception why there were so many generals. 'And why not?' he answered, 'Sure some of their mothers were generals too.'

Personal divisions and loyalties certainly played a part in determining allegiances. So did ancient family feuds, as in parts of Kerry. But the main reason was ideological. Each side claimed to be the legitimate government. The Irregulars' argument was that once the Republic had been proclaimed in 1916 and confirmed by the Dail in 1919, with all deputies

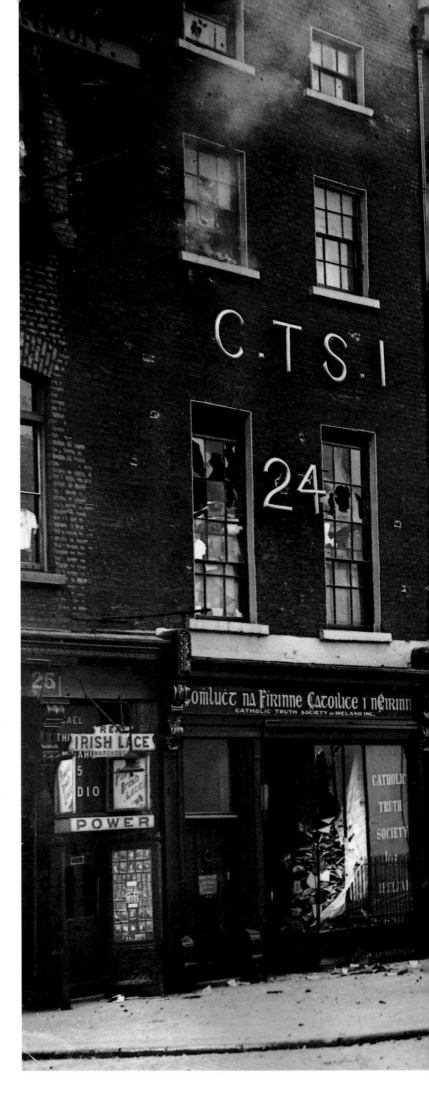

Easter week repeats itself, *as the Irregulars occupy buildings in central Dublin and the new Free State forces flush them out of each stronghold – just as in 1916. Much of* O'Connell Street was destroyed: here north Dublin's swankiest hotel, The Gresham, two doors down from the headquarters of the Catholic Truth Society of Ireland, burns freely.

Street fighting. *One of the two 18-pounder field-guns lent by the British to the Free State in action in O'Connell Street (above). Shards of glass fall from the shop window on the left, shattered by the muzzle flash of the gun. (Left) Free State snipers around a corner on St*

Stephen's Green. One fires as the other puts another clip of bullets into his magazine. Hostilities had opened with the Provisional Government attacking republicans in Dublin's Four Courts on 28 June 1922, using the same artillery lent by the British.

taking an oath of allegiance to it, then that was that. Subsequent votes in the Dail and the country in favour of the treaty were irrelevant. Nobody had the right to destroy the Republic. The Free State argument agreed that the Republic was the ideal, but the reality was that the British refused this status. Nevertheless they had conceded practical independence for Ireland; and the people, both in parliament and the country, had voted to accept this. Democracy must rule.

It took some time before the fighting started. Anti-treaty forces were strongest in the west and south-west, but one of their leaders, Rory O'Connor, seized the Four Courts in Dublin in April 1922. His men remained in possession, ignoring orders from the Provisional Government. Collins held off from confronting them, but eventually under strong pressure from the British (and borrowing some artillery from them) he ordered Dalton to drive O'Connor out. So 1916 was replayed in Dublin. Once again guns shelled public buildings; once again those inside were dispersed, killed or surrendered. Much of O'Connell Street was destroyed, and, as in 1916, the battle lasted a week. Those killed numbered 64, including Cathal Brugha, taking part in a suicide charge. In an explosion at the Four Courts, the country's historical records were blasted into the atmosphere; for days after blackened fragments rained down upon Dubliners. Collins would have agreed with Churchill's reaction in the House of Commons: 'Better a State without archives than archives without a State.'

The war then moved to the countryside. As in 1919–21, there were no real fronts, although the republicans did enjoy widespread control in the south-west. The campaign was fought around possession of key towns and barracks. Free State forces were largely in uniform, Irregulars usually in civilian clothes; but they were many exceptions on both sides. The result was a mobile, messy guerrilla conflict. Towns were gained, then lost; troops swore allegiance, then reneged. Free Staters were better armed, not only with artillery, but with what became the war-winning weapon – armoured cars. These were so rare they bore personal names: The Manager, The Fighting Second, The Custom House, Dublin Liz, Slievenamon – the last-named in the convoy carrying Michael Collins to his death. The Irregulars managed to capture one car, Balinalee, which boosted their activities around Sligo in the

early months, but mostly they were driven to construct their own unwieldy monsters, such as The River Lee, in essence an armour-plated lorry. Sean Hendrick, with the republicans in County Cork, remembers another home-built armoured car, which failed to arrive in an attack because it had no reverse gear and was driven by a Galway man who had to rely on a guide who stuttered and hence kept missing turnings.

Most of the country remained uninvolved and went about its business – as indeed it had done during the Anglo-Irish war. Many areas witnessed a sort of shadow boxing between the two forces: a ritual exchange of shots deliberately fired high and then withdrawal, usually by the Irregulars. In the early days of the Civil War, men were reluctant to kill fellow Irishmen, content to make an anti-treaty protest and no more. Civilities were maintained in the strangest of circumstances.

'There was a battle on the lawn this morning', reported Lady Susan Dawnay's gardener to her in a letter. 'There were no casualties and both sides greatly admired your Ladyship's antirrhinums.'

The phoney war suited Collins, who in the months immediately after the Treaty was preoccupied with the North. There the two sectarian communities were attacking each other, with the catholic minority in Belfast receiving the brunt. Thousands were driven from their jobs; hundreds of families burnt out; many killed. Over 250 violent deaths were recorded in the North in the first six months of 1922; protestants notched up four catholic murders to every one by catholics. Perpetrators were not just protestant mobs but a new force of part-time police, the B Specials, 48,000 strong and very partisan. A number of options were floated, and tried, including a secret understanding between Collins and elements of the IRA in Ulster, in order to protect northern catholics. Naturally this IRA activity, which included terrorising protestants in the border areas, was condemned by London, although Lloyd George was somewhat taken aback – 'a most extraordinary suggestion' – when Griffith and Collins demanded he declare martial law in Ulster and send in British troops which would have the confi-dence of the catholic community. In the event Collins and Craig hammered out a pact and the violence subsided.

As for the Boundary Commission, which was supposed to redraw the border between Northern Ireland and the Irish Free State on the principle of self-determination, it did not meet until 1924–25. Despite the boycott of the Commission by the Northern Ireland government, which of course stood to lose considerable territory if not entire counties, the unionist representative on it and a South African judge who was the supposedly neutral chairman (both appointed by Britain) decided to transfer only small portions of land from Northern Ireland; and even arranged for some southern land to go to the north. In desperation, the Irish representative resigned before the Commission published; and both southern and northern governments hurriedly confirmed the border as it was – the six counties partitioned from the rest of Ireland in 1920.

What Collins would have said to that will never be known for he was consumed by the Civil War three years earlier. By the summer of 1922 the Irregulars were largely contained in the south-west behind a line running from Limerick to Waterford. Both cities were taken by the Free State in July and the noose tightened on 'the Munster Republic'. In August Dalton captured Cork using strong nerves and a sea-borne force. The Irregulars did not give up, however, and moved to the countryside under the command of Liam Lynch, especially the Cork–Kerry border. They adopted the old guerrilla tactics of hit and run; roads were blocked by trees and mines; bridges blown; ambushes made.

War in the countryside, *though it did not always show: dancing in the roads continues at Glendalough. Irregulars (below) admire their* *handiwork prior to an ambush or just simple disruption to the traffic; the wise motorist now carried an axe and a saw in the boot.*

It was one such ambush in mid Cork which did for Michael Collins on 22 August. When the news reached Dublin, General Richard Mulcahy issued a fine message to the army: 'Stand by your posts. Bend bravely and undaunted to your work. Let no cruel act of reprisal blemish your bright honour ...' Perhaps the last word on Collins should be left to his enemy Eamon de Valera, who right at the end of his own long and distinguished career admitted: 'It is my considered opinion that in the full-ness of time history will record the greatness of Collins and it will be recorded at my expense.' Despite Mulcahy's plea the war now entered an increasingly vile, desperate stage. Arthur Griffith had died – ill for many months and worn out by

The Commander-in-Chief *of the Free State army, Michael Collins, lies in state (above) mourned by his brother John. He had been killed in an ambush near to his homeland in County Cork, diverted, in fact, from his inspection route by felled trees (see previous page) to the narrow valley of Beal na Blath.*

A chivalrous gesture. *British NCOs leave their barracks – for many troops had yet to be trans-ported home – and join the queue (above right) to pay their respects to their former enemy.*
[PHOTOS: JOSEPH CASHMAN]

events – a few weeks ahead of Collins. He was replaced by William Cosgrave and Mulcahy replaced Collins as commander-in-chief of the army. Soon there was a new graffito in Dublin: 'Move over Mick, make room for Dick, and Willie follows after.'

The new men determined to stamp out resistance. Draconian laws were introduced; one such was used to execute Erskine Childers on a technicality. When captured he had in his possession a tiny, ornamental revolver, given to him by Michael Collins in the old days; that proved enough for the death sentence. He was granted an hour's postponement of his execution so that he could see the sun come up once more,

and shook hands with each member of the firing squad. When the new Dail and Senate under the Free State constitution were established in December 1922, diehard republicans made it clear they would regard any officials as legitimate targets. After one Deputy was shot, the government, urged by the new strong man, Kevin O'Higgins, retaliated by shooting four prisoners in reprisal – all senior figures, including Rory O'Connor who had been O'Higgins' best man at his wedding twelve months previously. Before the Civil War ended, 77 men were to be executed by the Free State and thousands more imprisoned. The Irregulars struck back by burning the country houses of Senators (37 of them) and prominent Anglo-

Irishmen. George Moore's family home, owned and lived in by his brother, a Senator, went up in flames; as did Sir Horace Plunkett's house, another name from the Yeats' circle in the 1900s. Yeats himself was one of the new Senators; a fellow-Senator and friend, Oliver St John Gogarty (surgeon, florid wit and model for Joyce's Buck Mulligan) was captured and escaped by diving into the Liffey. Inevitably Gogarty's house too was burnt. Perhaps 200 Big Houses were destroyed from 1919 to 1923, most of them in the Civil War.

The worst human atrocities occurred in Kerry. Mines were strewn by the Irregulars, often with a trigger mine beneath which went off when the first was cleared. Ghastly reprisals were taken, as at Ballyseedy when nine men were roped to a

Burning the Big Houses. *Among those torched by republicans in the Civil War was Kilteragh, the newly built home of Sir Horace Plunkett, creator of the Co-operative Movement, and tireless reformer for Ireland. On the right the ruins of Tyrone House, long deserted by the St George family, but burnt nonetheless. The Fitzgeralds of Carton, County Kildare, were spared a burn-out when locals reminded the Irregulars that the house was the birthplace of Lord Edward Fitzgerald, hero of the 1798 rising.*

log and a mine then exploded. Eventually an inquiry was held and the Free State General Daly relieved of his command. He commented, 'No-one told me to bring kid gloves, so I didn't.'

By the spring of 1923 it was clear to even the diehards that

Horse Show Week *at Ballsbridge, Dublin, was well attended in August 1922 (above) though there were no entries from the North since the republicans held the road at Dundalk; Trinity College 'rag week' (top) went about its business in June 1922, ignoring the approaching hostilities in Dublin; (right) the singer Count John McCormack admires his portrait by the Irish painter Sir William Orpen, which hung at Moore Abbey, the imposing pile rented by McCormack from the Earl of Drogheda in the 1920s.*

Relief on the faces *in this Dublin crowd at College Green as it cheers W. T. Cosgrave on his election victory as President of the Executive Council of the Free State (in effect Prime Minister) in August 1923. His audience here are not really interested in Oaths, Republics, External Association and such constitutional niceties – all they yearn for is peace. Cosgrave was the leader and founder of Cumann na nGaedheal which ruled Ireland until 1932; he practised rigid conservatism in the social and economic spheres, while scrupulously observing the terms of the Anglo-Irish Treaty.*

the game was up. For a guerrilla struggle to survive, the key prerequisite is a sympathetic population to shelter men in the field. The favourite analogy is Mao Tse-tung's fish and the water. The guerrillas themselves – the fish – are almost impossible to catch; but you can shrink the amount of water – the sympathetic population – in which they swim. Against the British – yes, the people would aid the boys and not inform, but against fellow-Irishmen – that was a different matter. The killing had to stop. The Church hierarchy and the bulk of the priesthood were solidly behind the Free State government. Until recently there were no reliable casualty figures for the war, and estimates ranged as high as 4,000 dead; but the number can now be established at just under 1,000 – fewer killed than in the War of Independence but still a fearful total.

In April Liam Lynch, the Irregulars' commander, was killed and his successors turned to de Valera as head of the 'Republican government' to announce a surrender. On 24 May 1923 the ceasefire came, but the republicans were told to hide their arms against the day when the fight for the true Republic was resumed. To this extent the Civil War was never declared finished. In time this advice would come back to haunt de Valera.

The **Free State strong man,** *Kevin O'Higgins (left, with his wife at the races), excited particular detestation among republican die-hards and he was eventually assassinated in 1927. At his funeral Tim Healy, the Free State's first Governor-General (an astonishing conclusion to a maverick career) marches with Cosgrave (below right). Healy's crushed expression betrays his despair at the endless killing of Irishmen by Irishmen.*

De Valera's son *(above) speaks to a rally on behalf of his imprisoned father. Republicans refused to accept the new state and some prominent members were gaoled.*
[ALL PHOTOS: JOSEPH CASHMAN]

CHAPTER SIX

INDEPENDENT IRELAND

The horse's day *was well and truly over by the time this quaint scene was captured in a snowy Dublin, in the early 1980s. This winter load in front of City Hall, being pulled by a stoical nag, might have been commonplace in the late 1950s and early 1960s but things had then changed fast, especially once Ireland was in the European Union after 1973. It might suit the Tourist Board to pretend otherwise, but the country was catching up with the 20th century in a rush.* [PHOTO: ANDY FARREN]

IN SEPTEMBER 1997 THE BBC SOAP SERIAL, *Eastenders*, moved its location away from friendly, grotty Albert Square in east London, over to Ireland for three episodes. Much of the action took place in a house swarming with children and featuring a drunken husband. Outside in the town's streets, sheep, cows and donkeys outnumbered vehicles, the local pub harboured aggressive, neanderthal inmates, poverty lurked everywhere.

The strongly created impression was of an Ireland primitive, violent and distinctly behind the times. The reaction from Irish people and those who know the country in the 1990s was not only annoyance but amused surprise that the old stereotype could be recycled so unthinkingly. For modern Ireland is light years away from from such easy, patronising generalisations. Thirty years ago, however, such a crude picture would have done little injustice to much of southern Ireland.

The theme of independent Ireland during those forty years, from its birth in the 1920s to the eventual breakthrough to European prosperity in the 1970s, can be stated as social and economic continuity. In the 1950s the country looked much like it had in the 1920s. Horse-drawn vehicles were not uncommon, even in towns. In Dublin, electric trams ran until 1949. In the countryside donkey carts, with one or two milk churns balanced behind the driver on their way to the creamery, could still be seen well into the 1960s. Cars were chased along roads by suicidal sheep dogs. Ireland in the 1920s was a poor country but not greatly behind other European countries or even Britain. By the end of this period, however, it was to record the lowest living standards, the worst unemployment rates and the highest emigration figures in northern Europe. During the late 1930s and 1940s its citizens had less than half the wealth per capita of Britain – and it showed. Shaming comparisons were made with Denmark, which had roughly the same population and a similar agricultural economy. Closer by far were Iberian or southern Mediterranean countries such as Portugal or Greece – but these, at least, had some decent weather.

If material welfare was the issue, then Ireland from the 1920s to the 1960s was not the place to be. The ageing revolutionary S. P. Irwin summed it up in a heartfelt outburst: 'Although we freed ourselves from the British, we did not acquire for ourselves British freedom … whilst in the same period Britain shed her empire, became humanitarian, set up the welfare state and became socialistic, we have clung to the

The Church triumphant.

The Catholic Church was an integral part of the fabric of the Republic's daily life. Mothers wanted their sons to 'take up the cloth' as here (above), a group playing a less than saintly hand of cards on Lough Gill in 1933. Fr. Browne S. J. introduces schoolboys to the mysteries of God and to his dead uncle, Robert Browne, Bishop of Cloyne. In the same year de Valera kneels to kiss the ring of the Archbishop of Dublin (right).
[PHOTOS, TOP LEFT AND RIGHT: FR. BROWNE S. J.]

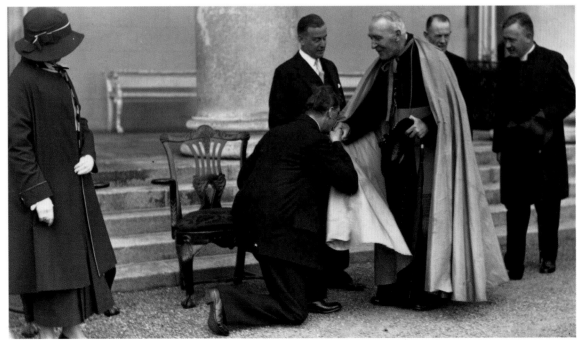

outworn and outdated conservative attitude which the British held forty years ago.' And it was not just material poverty but, for some, cultural deprivation as well. During those years Ireland was insulated and isolated. The Church was in its pomp and element – controlling education, censoring, blocking welfare progress, deadening the spirit of individuality. Many chafed at the restrictions but most felt little could be done: one simply put up with it like the weather. A French film producer in the early 1960s could remark: 'This seems to be a country led by old people in all spheres. Your young people know this and feel they cannot fight against it.'

There was no real mystery why poverty should have been so evident. Ireland was predominently an agricultural country, stuck on the edge of Europe, with few natural resources. Well over half the workforce were engaged on the land in the 1920s. Because of the 19th-century land purchase acts, already most of the land before independence was owner-occupied; and the 1923 Land Act provided for the compulsory purchase of all remaining leasehold land. As is well known – in rural France, the Balkans as well as Ireland – there is no more aboriginal conservative being than the peasant proprietor. Most of the farms were small, many so tiny as to be uneconomical: in 1931 only 9 per cent were over 100 acres and 31 per cent bigger than 15 acres.

If poverty was bad in the countryside it could be worse in the towns. In 1961, 43 per cent of all private dwellings were without piped water, while 35 per cent had no lavatory. The German novelist, Heinrich Boll, remembers coming to Ireland in the early 1950s and being struck by the use of the safety pin to hold clothes together. Health services for the poor were exiguous and often humiliating to obtain. In one dreadful case in 1927 a family practically starved to death – father, mother, two of the five children dead when discovered.

The government's attitude to social welfare was rigidly conservative and little was done in deference to the fears of property owners about taxes, and the sacred operation of the free

The politicians *were no doubt happy to have the great excavations for the Shannon hydroelectric scheme portrayed in oils by Socialist Sean Keating, adopting a suitably heroic pose as he paints (right), but many urban scenes were of unrelieved and unpicturesque poverty. In the countryside there were roofless houses aplenty, abandoned by those forced to emigrate in search of work. All over the world, from Soviet Russia to New Deal America, governments loved hydroelectric schemes because they were big and photogenic, and lent themselves to boasting that covered up failures at grassroots level, like this view on the outskirts of Cork in the 1930s (left).*
[PHOTO, LEFT: FR. BROWNE S. J.]
[PHOTO, RIGHT: JOSEPH CASHMAN]

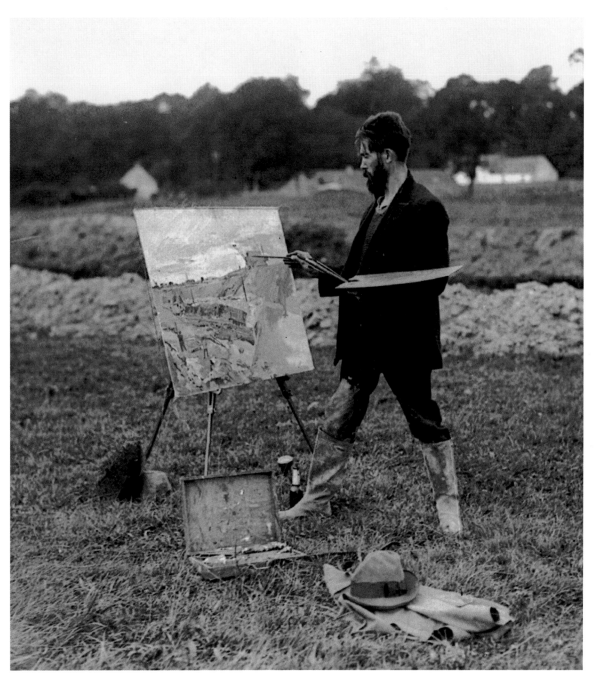

market. In fact, the old-age pension was cut by a shilling a week in 1924. Benefits introduced in Britain, especially after the Second World War, remained unknown in Ireland. It is true there occurred the Electrification of the Irish Free State (complete with a suitably Soviet Realist-style painting by Sean Keating) with the Shannon hydroelectric scheme in 1925, which led to the establishment of the Electricity Supply Board – but this was an exceptional venture. Matters were not helped by a trade war with Britain from 1932 to 1938. On coming to power de Valera refused to forward the land annuities to the British government (those financial installments paid annually by ex-tenants to the government as ordained in the various land acts and endorsed by the 1921 Treaty) and the British had responded by tariffs on Irish exports. The Irish reciprocated; but since 96 per cent of exports went to Britain it is hardly surprising that the effects on the home economy were severe. The effort to find new markets was unsuccessful and

cattle production in particular suffered. It was about this time that Ireland's income per head fell to half that in Britain.

What could be done? With her tiny internal market, with very limited resources, and with all governments obediently following the instructions of the Merrion Street mandarins in the Finance Ministry to rule out borrowing, economic stagnation seemed set for good. The answer for many could only be emigration, thus continuing a process which had started after the Famine. This was a national haemorrhage, which embarrassed and saddened some patriots, but it was also the safety valve which allowed Ireland's survival. In demographic terms, Ireland was exceptional for over 100 years. Most European countries saw their populations grow – apart from the positive checks of war – from the 1850s to the 1960s; in Ireland numbers dropped from 8 million plus before the Famine to $4^{1}/_{4}$ million in the 1950s, of which 3 million were in the south. (This was to fall to 2.8 million by 1961.) Rural depopulation, particularly

Road bowling. *Young boys (right) try their hand at a very grown-up sport in Tipperary, probably the oldest indigenous one in Ireland. A 28-ounce round shot is thrown down a course, which is also a road, two to three miles long, often between two villages, and incorporating a couple of good corners. Whoever takes the least number of throws is the winner. Those who have put money on a particular player will go on ahead to advise him on the best line.*

Kissing the Blarney Stone. *Two young girls (left) nervously await their turn at Blarney Castle in 1955. They will need all the chatty charm they can get if they are to catch Mr Right and avoid a late marriage to the wrong man, or even spinsterhood – all too normal in rural Ireland at the time.*

in the west, stripped the countryside bare. Ruined villages – gables and walls standing, roofs long gone – were everywhere, though most had already been abandoned in the later 19th century. Whole communities upped and went. The fate of a class of boys who left a national school in Mayo in 1944 makes a random illustration of the drain away from the homeland: in 1967, 12 of the 22 were overseas (6 in America, 4 in London); another 7 elsewhere in Ireland (5 in Dublin); only 3 were still living in their home town.

The emotional wrench must have been enormous, but regarded as inevitable and to be endured. Boll sees little Pedar or Patrick 'aged 14, carrying his cardboard suitcase, hung about with medallions, supplied with a package of extra-thick sandwiches, embraced by his sobbing mother, stand at the bus stop to begin the great journey to Cleveland, Ohio, to Manchester, Liverpool, London or Sydney, to some uncle, a cousin, a brother perhaps, who has promised to look after him and do something for him …' Most rural families saw the majority of their children leave the locality. Families, though large, might have been larger still had it not been for the high age of marriage: in 1929 the highest in the world, being 30 for women and 35 for men. The eldest son, ready to take over the farm, could not do so, or easily marry, until his father retired –

Dancing at a crossroads *in Connemara in about 1955. The square formed by two roads was a good enough place to meet and have a dance with the locals. In isolated areas it was often the only place.* [PHOTO: G. A. DUNCAN]

Murphy Brown, *a local road bowling champion, has just let fly near Blarney in the 1930s. Here are the boys of earlier years, perhaps become lonely rural bachelors. The sport is still popular, particularly in the north and south-west, in counties Armagh and Cork.*

not a speedy matter since one-third of all farmers in 1946 were over 65 years of age. Hence the phenomenon of the rural bachelor, and lonely hearts advertisments which began 'Youth, aged 44, desires wife …' It may have been hard for the men, but it could be much worse for the women. Those who did marry often ended up with far older and correspondingly non-sympatico husbands; or, as in William Trevor's classic story 'The Ballroom of Romance', were doomed to disappointment and hopeless compromises. Boys would tend to emigrate when leaving the locality; girls often went to the cities, particularly Dublin, some to disport themselves and find their 'Mr Gentleman' as Edna O'Brien heroines do in *The Country Girls*.

Substantial numbers of the Anglo-Irish departed after the Treaty, but many hung on, their world picture undisturbed by any mere political change. For these stalwarts 'the government' and the 'services' did not mean anything happening in Dublin; independent Ireland simply did not exist. Their children continued to be educated in England; perhaps took in four years' hard drinking at Trinity College, Dublin; and then departed once again for the British colonial service or Army. Letters were still addressed to Lower Sackville Street instead of O'Connell Street in Dublin (and were delivered); tickets to Kingstown instead of Dun Laoghaire were requested on trains

The Anglo-Irish *were still around in the 1950s, as here, though many had left in the 1920s. The Meath Hunt Ball gets down to serious wet napkin throwing at Dublin's Gresham Hotel, while the venerable party at the Kildare Hunt Ball seems sensibly to be running the roulette bank. The Kildare opening meet brings out the full sartorial range. The behaviour was not always rowdy; in local cinemas many Anglo-Irish would dutifully stand during the national anthem, 'The Soldier's Song', while the locals made an unseemly rush for the exit.*
[ALL PHOTOS: G. A. DUNCAN]

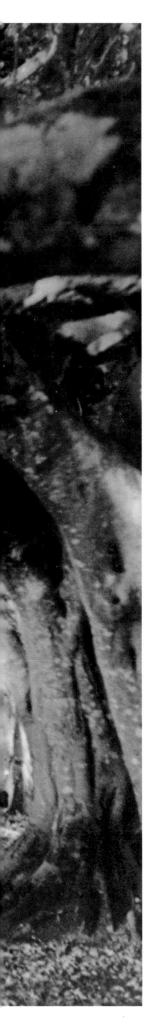

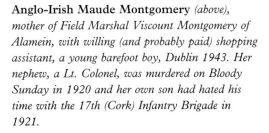

Anglo-Irish Maude Montgomery *(above),*
mother of Field Marshal Viscount Montgomery of
Alamein, with willing (and probably paid) shopping
assistant, a young barefoot boy, Dublin 1943. Her
nephew, a Lt. Colonel, was murdered on Bloody
Sunday in 1920 and her own son had hated his
time with the 17th (Cork) Infantry Brigade in
1921.

A pet pig called Venus *(above right) and its*
owner, Mrs Gerald Tenison of Lough Bawn,
County Monaghan, 1950.

French Park, County Roscommon. *The Hons.*
Hope and Prudence French, daughters of Lord De
Freyne, in the grounds of their beautiful 18th-
century family home (left), which was pulled down
soon after 1945 and its demesne parcelled out
among small farmers by the Land Commission.
The first De Freyne had come to Ireland with
Strongbow in 1170.
[PHOTO: FR. BROWNE S. J.]

(and provided); on the monarch's birthday Union Jacks would fly over remote demesnes. The rest of the country looked tolerantly on. After 1945 the traffic in gentry across the Irish Sea was temporarily reversed as a number of English ones, atavistically conservative, often catholic, and troubled by the reforms and taxes of the Labour government, moved to large houses in Ireland, a process known as The Flight from Moscow. Evelyn Waugh nearly joined this caravan, greatly taken with Gormanston Castle north of Dublin. Many of the large houses sprang leaks, crumbled, were sold to convents or entrepreneurs – as Bowen's Court was to a local man who demolished it.

The rural world celebrated its provincialism. '44 Pigs Drowned at Fermoy' was supposed to have been the headline in a north Cork paper the day the Japanese bombed Pearl Harbor. (If true, this was an interesting reversal of global pretensions: at the turn of the century another local Cork paper announced it had 'its eye on the Tsar of Russia'.) Hard work was not regarded with favour. 'If it's a great day for working then it's a great day for fishing.' Whitewashed stone cottages, with smoke curling from the chimneys, often had men propped like posts against the wall, hands in pockets, resting their minds. Commentators raged against the conservative mentality and destructive ignorance. The farmers, complained an expert as late as the 1960s, 'are a lot of bloody fellows who just don't want to be efficient. This could be a great farming country. We have some of the finest farmland in the world ... but the average farmer isn't really interested in doing better. He grumbles all the time but what he really cares about is the amount of time he can spend drinking with the lads.' Co-operative ventures to share machinery were rare. 'Not those bloody fellows', said a parish priest in Kerry, 'the first sunny day and they'll be fighting with each other to see who gets to use the tractor first.' Days in the towns as well as the countryside started late, to the bemusement of foreigners trying to get to banks or arrange appointments. The definition of a gentleman in Ireland was thought to be someone who did not have to get up in the morning – and a great deal of Irishmen considered themselves to be gentlemen.

Although emigration distressed everybody, poverty was seen to have its advantages. The consequent lack of materialism proved congenial to certain minds, principally de Valera's. In 1943 he rejoiced in an 'ideal Ireland … the home of a people who valued material wealth only as the basis of right living, of a people who were satisfied with frugal comfort and devoted their leisure to the things of the spirit … The Irish genius has always stressed spiritual and intellectual rather than material values.' In practical terms this meant recognising and supporting the predominant position of the Church in Irish life.

Bird and beast. *Paddy Kilecourse, a chimney sweep, about to dangle his trained goose down a cottage chimney in 1955 (right). It flapped its wings, the soot was dislodged, and the job was done.*

Cattle are driven *to market (left) along the Stillorgan–Donnybrook Road, Dublin, 1958, and the bus just has to wait.*
[PHOTO: G. A. DUNCAN]

In the Irish constitution of 1937, article 44.1, a special position was accorded the Catholic Church 'as the guardian of the faith professed by the great majority of the citizens'. In literal terms this meant little except the recognition of an obvious fact; but symbolically it signified that the Irish state would be sensitive and responsive to catholic demands. In practical matters this ensured that the Church would continue its control over the national schools and, more importantly, exert an undefined influence over social policy – not only on issues such as divorce, but social welfare and censorship.

The position of the Catholic Church in Ireland is a contentious subject, even today when much of the medieval lumber and deference has been swept away. Unlike European catholic countries (except Poland) Irish catholics are very much a practising people, with churches packed on Sundays and holy days of obligation. Before the 1960s the Church's power was upheld by politicians of all nationalist persuasions. The Eucharistic Congress of 1932 offered the new party, Fianna Fail, the chance to establish its fidelity – after the embarrassing moment during the Civil War when the hierarchy had come out against the anti-Treaty forces and de Valera himself excommunicated. Fianna Fail was only catching up Cosgrave's pro-Treaty party which had obediently outlawed divorce in 1923, despite the olympian objections of W. B. Yeats on behalf of his fellow protestants: 'We against whom you have done this thing are no petty people. We are one of the great stocks of Europe. We are the people of Burke: we are the people of Grattan; we are the people of Swift, the people of Emmet, the people of Parnell. We have created most of the modern literature of this country. We have created the best of its political intelligence.' Magnificent stuff – but not exactly the sort of remarks designed to ingratiate himself with his non Anglo-Irish audience.

Protestants who did remain in the south found their numbers (if not their influence) declining, partly from emigration in the first few years but also because of the Papacy's *Ne Temere* decree, by which children of a mixed marriage were to be brought up catholics. The Church took a strong line in defence of this right, and in 1957 the hierarchy endorsed a boycott of protestants in Fethard-on-Sea, County Wexford, for the crime of a mixed marriage couple choosing to have their children educated at a protestant school. Such was the prevailing mood of the times that Hubert Butler, when writing to protest to *The Irish Times*, 'wrote anonymously, as one often did in the Fifties', as he recalled in 1978. In some cases the hierarchy was largely bluster and no bite. Trinity College, Dublin, was stigmatised as a godless institution by some bishops, most notably Archbishop John Charles McQuaid, and until the early 1970s catholics forbidden to study there; but thousands ignored such agonised advice, treating it merely as an arch-reactionary's foible. Catholics from abroad were completely unaware of the ban.

Swimming a horse *out to the waiting steamer, where it would be winched aboard using the improvised rope harness round its body, then transported to the mainland. This kind of scene, in 1954, was the inspiration for Robert Flaherty's famous film,* Men of Aran, *made in 1934. It was said the islanders would not learn to swim, believing that, once embraced by the waves, 'the sea must not be denied'.*
[PHOTO: G. A. DUNCAN]

But the Church did demonstrate its strength over the more vital matter of social welfare: none more so than in the Mother and Child scheme of 1951. This provided for a state maternity health programme to operate without a means test; in truth a moderate proposal and no way approaching the full provisions of Britain's newly established National Health Service. The project was introduced by Noel Browne, the only minister in the new coalition government who would not have objected to being called a socialist. Already Browne had done wonders in practically eradicating TB, which had lingered in Ireland longer than other European countries. But his new plan came up against not only predictable opposition from the doctors (diagnosing that dreaded virus, socialised medicine) but the catholic hierarchy who feared an invasion of family rights and the possibility of sex education. Once there was the threat of the croziers starting to swing there could only be one outcome, although the Church did not have to commit any public action, relying, with justifiable confidence, on Browne's colleagues to scotch the scheme and sack the peccant minister. All might have been smoothed over, but Browne had the bad manners to

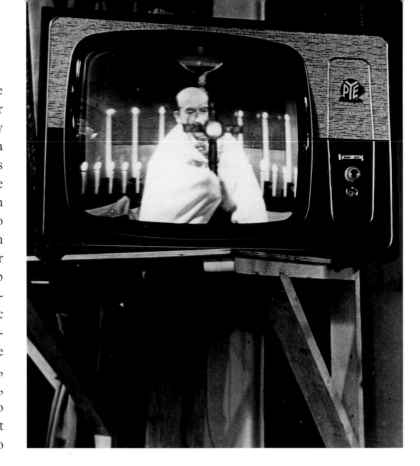

Television arrives *in 1961, in spite of the deep suspicions of the Church. Following the dictum, 'If you can't ban it, bless it', Archbishop McQuaid did just that in its opening moments (above). Patrick O'Hagan sang to a Dublin crowd, who could 'see themselves on the tele', if they had good enough eyesight, on the one set provided (right). Shirt, tie and jacket were obviously de rigueur for the directing staff (left).*

publish the correspondence between himself and the bishops. The provision of general benefits and social welfare approximating to those in northern Europe had to wait for the more prosperous, and in cultural terms more open, times of the 1970s.

Many women at this time were repressed and ignored throughout much of Europe, not just Ireland. But the Church's pervasive influence there made it particularly hard to challenge its dominant vision. 'The idea that it was desirable for all women to go off for their lifetime with one man and have his children as their life's task was completely uncriticised.' Another voice from the 1960s pointed out: 'There's no life for a woman here outside of marriage. It's the be-all and end-all. This is a terrible country for a single woman, and especially in Dublin where there are so many more women than men.'

Those that did marry then had the prospect of endless children: in the mid 1960s the fertility rate was more than twice that of Britain or America. A fifth of all Irish mothers had seven or more children; some 6,000 in 1966 had twelve or more. The exhausting struggle to make ends meet often led to illness and breakdowns. The Church's support was unappreciated. One mother of numerous children, after listening to a Franciscan preaching on matrimony, left the hall remarking 'I wish to God I knew as little about it as that one.' It was a very long time before contraception was to become freely available in the south – only in the last ten years or so. Women's groups would make well publicised visits to the North, waving blown up condoms on their return. An attempt was made by the coalition government to legalise contraception in 1974, but the bill failed to pass the Dail after a number of deputies, including

Gypsies in their best. *A family from Buttevant, County Cork, on their way to Cahirmee Fair in the late 1950s (left). Families of six and more were far from rare but any attempts at introducing contraception were stifled by clerical opposition.*
[PHOTO: ELINOR WILTSHIRE]

Before his time. *Noel Browne, seen above in retirement playing his accordion, had bravely tried to introduce a state scheme, during his time as a government minister, for the health of mothers and children. A combination of doctors in fear of socialised medicine and priests in fear of the spread of sexual enlightenment killed the programme and got Browne thrown out of the government.*
[PHOTO: BOBBY HANVEY]

the Taoiseach of the day, voted against it. Mental illnesses were prevalent during these forty years. Madness, of course, has had a long pedigree in Ireland, first marked, perhaps, from Swift's donation in 1725:

> *He gave the little wealth he had*
> *To build a house for fools and mad,*
> *And showed by one satiric touch,*
> *No nation needed it so much.*

In the mid 1960s nearly half the hospital beds in Ireland were occupied by mental patients. Anxious not to be thought too socialist, various governments did little to take control of mental health, allowing the religious orders and charity to bear the main burden.

It sounds a record of unrelieved gloom, but this would be a misleading conclusion: it was simply that the great majority of Irish people at this time had priorities different from those common elsewhere; it was also a deliberate attempt to distance themselves from the overriding influence of the neighbouring big island. Ireland might have achieved independence from a grudging Britain but, unless it could practise its own customs and find its own culture, it would remain an appendage. In part this explains the support given to the Irish language. After the Famine, it had died out almost in a generation, and although the Gaelic Revival of the 1890s and 1900s pushed life back into the corpse, it was very much a minority practice by 1921. Patrick Pearse had proclaimed that Ireland would never

truly be free until it was Gaelic, and subsequent nationalists, particularly de Valera, were to echo him. 'I believe that as long as the language remains you have a distinguishing characteristic of nationality which will enable the nation to persist. If you lose the language the danger is absorption.' In the 1920s Irish became the medium for infant classes and a compulsory subject in secondary schools; in the 1930s a pass in Irish was essential to gain any credits in the school-leaving examinations; for various official posts some proficiency in Irish was mandatory. In the 1937 Constitution Irish was proclaimed the first official language of the state, the use of English as a second language pragmatically being added.

The healthy resistance of the Irish to being forced to do anything meant the policy had only mixed success. Many learnt it reluctantly at school and then promptly forgot it in the manner of children losing their French or German. There could be embarrassing moments when the first language was used by a deputy in the Dail, silencing normally verbose opponents, or idiotic moments when Irish subtitles were used for foreign films on television in the early days of RTE. Many came to realise that the dream of an Irish-speaking nation was impractical considering its nearness to Britain and the inexorable advance of Anglo-Saxon culture. Foreign commentators, and some Irishmen themselves, liked to prick the bubble of self-deception which they imagined this language policy entailed; but it could be argued that without such defence Irish might have disappeared entirely. As it was, special areas were designated Gaeltacht (large sections of counties Galway, Donegal

Literary lights. *Edna O'Brien (far left), before she had taken on a metropolitan gloss in London. Brian O'Nolan/Flann O'Brien/Myles na Gopaleen in the Palace Bar, Dublin, or what can be seen of him between hat and coat collar (above left). Samuel Beckett (above); awarded the* *Nobel Prize for Literature in 1970, he grunted 'catastrophe' and absconded to Tunisia; Michael Mac Liammoir (above right) at the keyboard prepares to soothe the savage breast of Brendan Behan, on the right. Behind Mac Liammoir, Hilton Edwards smokes his pipe.*

and Kerry, and isolated pockets elsewhere) and with material help the language flourished in these remote corners. The belief that the only true Irishman was an Irish speaker did continue (and is not unknown today) but many took a relaxed view of the business, best summarised by Myles na Gopaleen in the 1940s: 'I am in favour of the cultivation of the Irish language because it is ancient, beautiful and very interesting … but the modest proposal to revive Irish as the common everyday language … is arrant nonsense … English is a world language and we are lucky to have it, particularly as we have embroidered it with the tweedy fol-de-lols and porter stains which are unmistakenly Irish and proud of it.' What does puzzle still is the strength of Welsh compared to the Gaelic in Ireland and Scotland – and yet Welsh nationalism is by far the weakest of these Celtic strains. One part of Ireland where Gaelic literature not only survived but became celebrated was the Blasket Islands: the autobiographical accounts of Maurice O'Sullivan, Thomas O'Crohan and Peig Sayers proved an

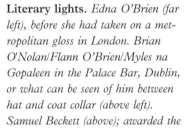

astonishing array of talent from a minuscule community.

Those Irishmen who embroidered the English language during this period included the towering figures of Joyce, Beckett and Yeats, although the former two were exiles, of course, and the latter, after a playing his part 'of a sixty-year-old smiling public man', moved into internal exile in the 1930s as well as spending much of his last decade abroad. Other Irish figures emigrated as well, including Sean O'Casey after *The Silver Tassie* had been turned down by the Abbey ('it takes courage and patience to live in Ireland' was his rueful conclusion), while ostensibly Irish writers, such as Louis MacNeice and Elizabeth Bowen spent their productive years in England. Those luminaries who remained in Ireland found the going tough because of the censorship of the period, which reached its height in the 1940s and 1950s. Almost any Irish writer of note had one or more of their works banned, including O'Casey, Beckett, Sean O'Faolain, Brendan Behan (who used to bellow when drunk 'I've banned the censorship board and there's no appeal against my decision'), Frank O'Connor and Edna O'Brien. (Strangely enough Joyce was not banned, perhaps because *Ulysses* was unpublished also in Britain and America.) As for world authors, the list is practically a roll-call of international heavyweights: seemingly most Frenchmen – Voltaire, Zola, Flaubert, Balzac, Proust, Sartre, de Maupassant – Hemingway, Fitzgerald, Salinger, Orwell, Huxley, Dylan Thomas – and Plato (for the *Symposium*). And this is only a tiny selection; in the 1950s about 600 books (mostly genuine rubbish) were being banned each year.

storyteller and his wife forced by bullying clerics to go down on their knees, literally, and condemn the book.

Part of intellectual life in the 1940s and 1950s centred around the periodical *The Bell*, edited by Sean O'Faolain and then Peadar O'Donnell. Among those who wrote for it were the essayist Hubert Butler, the poet Patrick Kavanagh (never without his uniform of broad-brimmed hat), and Frank O'Connor, the short story supremo. Kavanagh is generally recognised as the foremost poet in Ireland between Yeats and the rise of the northern poets in the 1960s, though he would have vigorously objected to being 'placed' in any poetic tradition. Much intellectual life existed in the various Dublin pubs, particularly the Palace Bar, the Pearl Bar and McDaid's. According to John Ryan, a patron figure for impecunious writers during this period, most of the literary Dubliners had a drinking problem – they couldn't get enough of it. Those whose reputations have lasted the years include Brendan Behan who, after serving time in borstal in England and prison in Ireland for IRA activities, wrote two classic plays and an autobiography, besides spending his last few years scandalising the Irish bourgeoisie and delighting his world-wide audience by

The Church was not directly responsible for the censorship, the initiative coming from laymen in the 1920s. Advocates formed pressure groups, such as the 'Irish Vigilance Association', and 'The Angelic Warfare for Maintaining the National Virtue of our Country'. W. B. Yeats once again intervened with superbly patrician advice: 'I think you can leave the arts, superior and inferior, to the general conscience of mankind', but was steamrollered aside. A censorship board was set up in 1930, acting on recommendations from a Committee of Enquiry on Evil Literature, and provision for censorship built into the 1937 Constitution. Although many writers took being banned in their stride – and indeed wore the rebuke as a badge of honour – there were some nasty cases, none more so than when Eric Cross' delightful book about a west Cork story-teller, *The Tailor and Ansty*, was banned, and the eponymous

Greasepaint and oils. *Sioban McKenna (far left) at an early rehearsal of a Sean O'Casey play. Cyril Cusack the actor (below left), all tweed and eyebrows; Jack B. Yeats (left), fated to be known as the brother of the poet W. B., yet Ireland's premier painter in his own right; Sean O'Sullivan (below right) contemplates his portrait of 'Dev'.*

This last mot was the favourite of the painter Sean O'Sullivan, but apart from the lonely eminence of Jack B. Yeats, the fine arts were less evident. Films were popular, but to see rather than produce. The high spot of a night out in Dublin was to queue for the pictures and then take your girlfriend to a mixed grill in the balcony restaurant. Touts used to patrol O'Connell Street offering cinema tickets to impatient first-nighters. Films themselves were censored, naturally, and some of those regarded as fit to be shown so riddled with cuts that the storyline became hard to follow. Audiences could be censored too – at least in Clones in 1943 where young men and women were forced to sit on opposite sides of the central aisle. The Abbey Theatre continued as the national forum but was now challenged by two Englishmen, Hilton Edwards (openly English) and Michael Mac Liammoir (bogusly Irish) who founded the Gate Theatre and produced several adventurous pieces. Denis Johnston's impressionist play, *The Old Lady Says No*, was one such which, under another title, had been rejected by the Abbey and returned to Johnston with that phrase written across the cover, the old lady being Augusta Gregory.

rumbustious public appearances. Interviewed by Malcolm Muggeridge on *Panorama*, he came over as more than half cut; questioned later whether he thought it was appropriate to appear drunk on the BBC, he replied: 'I thought it perfectly natural. Yes, in my case, yes.' Several times he invaded the West End theatre playing his *The Hostage*, once entertaining the queue outside with Irish songs, taking up a collection for the supplanted busker, yelling 'eejits' as the theatre audience stood to cheer him, and throughout the play interrupting with shouts of 'Up the rebels, up the Chinese'. Lately there has been some prurient interest about his sexuality – a notion which would have bored Behan, with his inclusive tolerance. When asked on American television if he was a practicising homosexual, he replied: 'I never knew you had to practise it. But if it's a choice between Whistler's mother, who is as ugly as sin, and Michelangelo's beautiful David, then there is no contest.'

Quarrels and backbiting were the order of the day. In 1952 Evelyn Waugh listened to a wireless programme celebrating George Moore's centenary. 'One after another the cracked old Irish voices took up the tale for nearly two hours, each demolishing bit by bit every corner of his reputation. That was Ireland alright.' Today Brian O'Nolan is probably the most esteemed of the Irish writers of this time, under his two pseudonyms of Flann O'Brien for the novels in English, and Myles na Gopaleen for his column in the *The Irish Times*. There were a host of other writers though not much actual writing got done. Behan's explanation was 'I am a drinker with a writing problem.' Such puns and witticisms were sometimes more prized than achieved works of art: 'Dublin is a city of spoiled Prousts', or 'We are the people our mothers warned us against.'

For some of the intelligentsia, the forty years after independence were miserable times; for others, incredibly intense. An acerbic English journalist, Honor Tracy, who had lived and worked in Ireland, summarised those days as mass in the morning, vacuity through the day, oblivion at night: religion, inertia, alcohol. Harold Pinter, on the other hand, maintained that 'Ireland wasn't golden always, but it was golden sometimes and in 1950 it was, all in all, a golden age for me and for others.'

Continuity there might have been in social and economic affairs, but these years were ones of political change. The basic direction was towards a greater detachment from Britain, chiselling away at the remaining links until complete and formal independence was achieved in 1949. Throughout the period (and beyond) the two major parties comprised those who had supported or rejected the Treaty of 1921. After the death of Collins and Griffith, W. T. Cosgrave took over as leader of the pro-Treaty faction, which in time evolved into Cumann na

Walking barefoot *(far left) round the crucifix, on a pilgrimage to Lough Derg, County Donegal.*

Through a glass darkly. *The reality of Irish bars and drinking habits a few decades ago (left and right), before the marketing men took hold and turned them into warm, soft-focus images to help sell a new generation of beers and stouts. Where's the craic here?*
[ALL PHOTOS: KLAUS FRANCKE]

nGaedheal (itself the forerunner of Fine Gael). To assert its authority was the new government's immediate task. In the 1923 election, de Valera's Sinn Fein had won 44 seats, and obedient to traditional tactics refused to sit in an 'usurping legislature', denying the legitimacy of the government. There was the constant risk of physical opposition, the government having to deal in 1924 with an incipient republican mutiny in the army. The strong man who dealt with this was Kevin O'Higgins and such was his legacy that his assassination in 1927 did not deflect the government from squaring up to recalcitrant elements of the old IRA.

By then, however, de Valera was back into constitutional politics. This meant being prepared to take the oath and thus break with the diehard element in Sinn Fein. By a process known only to himself, de Valera thereby accepted the Collins line in 1922: that the Treaty might be acceptable as an interim measure and stepping stone to greater constitutional independence in time. In 1932 there was much excitement when his new party, Fianna Fail ('warriors of destiny') won the election. Many on the pro-Treaty side had persuaded themselves that the new men were not only republican nationalists but communist fellow-travellers. When the new government took its seats in the Dail, some deputies carried pistols secreted in their clothing, though in the end none had to be drawn.

Roger Casement's *body brought back to Dublin (right) in 1965. Earlier, in 1947, Countess Markievicz's pistol and papers, captured by her cousin Captain De Courcy Wheeler in 1916, had come back, as had the green and gold flag that flew above the General Post Office.*

Removals. *Such gestures did not prevent the continued chiselling away of links with Britain: Queen Victoria on her way to retirement in 1948 (left). It was not until 1986 that she found a new home – ironically, Australia. Nelson's Pillar was blown up (above right) in 1966, despite having been paid for by public subscription back in 1808, long before his London column was erected. The magnificent William III on his horse outside Trinity had a less gentle exit; blown up in 1928, it was rumoured he was melted down to plug the holes in Dublin's decaying sewer pipes.*
[PHOTO, LEFT: G. A. DUNCAN]

During these years there was an element of street brawling between triumphalist republicans, some released by the new administration, and energetic members of the opposition. Taking a leaf out of European politics, some of the latter began to model themselves on Mussolini's fascist party. Under the leadership of the dismissed Police Commissioner, General O'Duffy, they acquired a uniform – blue not black – and in the next few years assumed some of the associated trappings – the hysterical anti-communism, the Roman salute, parades and even the awkward greeting of Hail O'Duffy. But in other respects the Blueshirts were weak stuff compared to the real fascist article and never openly adopted the policies advocated by Hitler and Mussolini, such as condemnation of democracy, imperialism and racism. For a year or so O'Duffy worked with assorted anti-Fianna Fail parties, but was expelled from constitutional politics in 1934. In 1936–37 he led 700 Blueshirts to Spain to fight for Franco (while 200 or so ex-IRA men fought for the Republicans).

The constitutional opponents to Fianna Fail had formed themselves into Fine Gael ('the tribe of the Irish') and in the 1930s emphasised general conservative virtues, law and order, the interests of the larger farmers, and keeping the tenuous links with the Empire. Naturally they attacked de Valera's trade war with Britain but perhaps to their surprise – and certainly the British goverment's – found that what might harm a people's economic advantage did not necessarily direct their political sympathies. For de Valera now proceeded to dismantle the constitution of the Free State in his search for unambiguous national sovereignty – and the Irish people very largely approved.

In part Ireland took advantage of the decentralisation of the British Commonwealth in the 1930s. (South Africa and Canada took the lead here, with Australia and New Zealand more Empire-conscious.) Ireland's dominion status had been

defined in the 1921 Treaty by explicit comparison with Canada. The statute of Wesminster in 1931 declared the dominions fully autonomous, though members of the Commonwealth, and that Britain could not legislate for them. This meant, in effect, that the dominions themselves could legislate at will – even to the extent of breaking any link with Britain. As far as Ireland was concerned Britain had now conceded the issue which had led to the Irish Civil War: a pity Lloyd George's government had not the foresight and imagination to occupy this position in 1921.

Once in power in 1932, de Valera immediately removed the oath of allegiance – his own particular bug-bear – and then produced Ireland's present constitution in 1937. The Free State now became Eire, the Irish for Ireland. Articles 2 and 3 – much discussed today – announced the national territory to be 'the whole island of Ireland' and the right of the Dublin parliament to exercise jurisdiction over it; though pragmatically it did add that 'pending the re-integration of the national territory' laws would apply only to the southern 26 counties. Strangely perhaps, de Valera did not take the final step and declare Ireland to be a Republic. His reasoning appeared to be a reluctance to dignify only three-quarters of Ireland with the name for which men had fought and died in 1916; and a hope that by keeping Ireland associated with the Commonwealth, the northern Unionists might feel moved to rejoin the south.

The question whether Ireland was inside or outside the Commonwealth continued to vex the experts. The Irish view was that Eire was outside and only externally associated; the

British view that Ireland was still a functioning member. The issue only became relevant on the outbreak of war in 1939 – and immediately the Irish view triumphed since Ireland was the only Commonwealth (or ex-Commonwealth) country to remain neutral.

Irish neutrality during the Second World War was not just popular, but a source of pride as well. It became the most visible proof that the country indeed was fully independent of Britain: 'neutrality is Eire's first free self-assertion', judged Elizabeth Bowen, the Anglo-Irish novelist who provided intelligence reports to the British government throughout the war. Many in England – not least Churchill – reacted grudgingly to such 'disloyalty', as they liked to term it; and Ireland's stance, in probably the most moral war for centuries, can look unattractive now. At that time, however, Irish eyes were not upon the global issue but upon Ireland's relationship with Britain. Considering the long sad record, and the more recent history of open Anglo-Irish hostilities, it had to be so.

Once announced, neutrality had to be defended. There were times, especially in 1940, when the country might have been invaded – by Germany or Britain. The British brought much pressure to bear for the Irish to return the Treaty ports, particularly Berehaven and Cobh in the south-west (returned, almost absentmindedly, to Ireland in 1938) in order to help their anti-submarine campaign in the Atlantic. De Valera saw this as making subsequent Irish neutrality impossible. Yet he might have considered such a move had the British pledged themselves to ending partition. Throughout the war years (and

The Spanish Civil War *had Irishmen on both sides, like Frank Ryan, IRA hardliner, posing with Spanish republican comrades (top left), or these volunteers (top right) returning after being wounded fighting for Franco and the fascists.*

Blueshirts on parade. *Mrs 'General' O'Neill, Kinsale, County Cork, 1933, with some reassuringly ill-drilled followers. Like the rest of Europe, Ireland was susceptible to extremist politics.*
[PHOTOS, TOP LEFT AND LEFT: MICHAEL MCINERNEY]

beyond) visitors to his office would be given the map treatment: shown a map of Ireland with Eire in black, the North 'a leprous white', while the Taoiseach would insist 'there's the real source of all our trouble'.

The war years were designated the Emergency, the government awarding itself total executive power. Public neutrality was administered impartially and rigorously – even to the extent of de Valera paying a courtesy call on the German representative at Hitler's death. Censorship was taken to the lengths of suppressing any news item which might reveal Irishmen serving in the British forces. The pro-British *Irish Times* once managed to get round this restriction by announcing that a former member of the paper who had joined the Royal Navy, and who had survived the sinking of his ship, was safe and sound after a 'boating accident in the Pacific'. Other casualties were referred to as 'in hospital suffering from lead poisoning incurred in the Libyan desert'. The editor drew attention to the fact that many Allied commanders in 1941 came from Ireland in the following manner. 'Mr Winston Churchill … mentioned by name nine military and naval commanders who had gained fame recently in North Africa and in the Mediterranean. I append the names of the gallant nine.

General Wavell	English
General Mackie	Australian
General Wilson	Japanese (North Island)
General O'Connor	Japanese
General O'Moore Creagh	Japanese
General Dill	Japanese (North Island)
General Brooke	Japanese (North Island)
Admiral Cunningham	Japanese
Admiral Somerville	Japanese.'

These examples may have been winked at by the censor, but the usual attitude was one of humourless rigidity. Once a picture of a pretty girl captioned 'Spring comes to St Stephen's

The Free State Army *(left) steps out in breeches and German-style coal-scuttle helmets, shouldering British Lee-Enfield rifles. The Army suffered shortages of weapons and equipment; some of the armoured cars were constructed by blacksmiths in Carlow using Ford chassis.*

The Air Force *(right) had a few Gloster Gladiator bi-planes, like this example having one of its machine-gun magazines loaded by its pilot.*

Green' was deleted on the grounds that the light summer dress might provide 'useful meteorological information to one or other of the combative forces'.

Very large numbers of southern Irishmen, in the region of 50,000, did volunteer for war service, more than from Northern Ireland, though precise figures are impossible to obtain (and disputed by embarrassed and enraged northern politicians). Privately, Irish officials gave valuable aid to the Allied side, from military intelligence to the silent transfer of stranded Allied air-crews to Northern Ireland. The southerners returned on leave, of course, but preserved the fiction of non-combatancy by changing into civilian clothes which the British considerately stored at the ports of Holyhead and Fishguard. 'There was no sensation of going to an ideologically-different country', remembers one such serviceman. 'It was as if the Allies had voluntarily set apart a region where steaks and drink and bright lights were provided – a kind of convalescent home.'

Britain's representative to Dublin was the impressive Sir John Maffey, six foot four high and the beau ideal of the colonial offical until his retirement as Governor-General of the Sudan in 1934. At the Dublin embassy he practised a rigorous defence of Britain's interests with some style and aplomb – amongst his more official duties he ran a cricket team which played in College Park. The German ambassador was Dr Edouard Hempel, unusually not a member of the Nazi party, and as shrewd as Maffey in summing up the situation in Ireland. Outside his legation at 58 Northumberland Road the Swastika flag flew every day. (Because of Ireland's ambiguous constitutional position in relation to Britain, Maffey was refused permission to fly the Union Jack.) On Maffey's staff was the poet John Betjeman who, in the intervals of visiting his favourite dilapidated Anglo-Irish mansions, occasionally signed letters as 'Sean O Betjemean, attache na press'. Betjeman had taken the measure of Ireland a few years before the war, writing to T. S. Eliot: 'Do you know Oireland? It is what England was like in the time of Rowlandson, with Roman Catholicism thrown in.'

One thing Betjeman enjoyed in Dublin was a plentiful supply of red meat. Rationing in Ireland took a strange shape. Meat and dairy products were fairly plentiful, but there were severe shortages of tea, half a pound of which would be swapped for a bottle of whiskey. Clothes and shoes were rationed; luckily Fianna Fail's drive for autarky in the 1930s now proved its worth. With no fuel resources, apart from peat, travel proved difficult. Petrol was reserved for essential purposes. Some cars were powered by gas which was stored in a lumpy balloon tethered to the roof, or in a unit towed behind the car in a trailer. Horses and a bizarre collection of vehicles came out of retirement. A twenty-seat stage coach was used in Limerick, while horse-drawn cabs appeared in Dublin. Bicycle theft became the new crime. The transport system struggled on but threw away any pretence of a timetable. 'There she comes! Right on the day!' enthused a railway porter in a *Dublin*

Wartime fuel rationing. *It was as well that Irish transport was so reliant on quadrupeds pre-war, with plenty of horse-drawn vehicles still around. These came into their own once petrol was scarce, like this overloaded jaunting car in central Dublin.*
[PHOTO: G. A. DUNCAN]

The scene in Cahir *in 1942 (right) is enough to make an ecologist dance for joy, but the picture was probably taken to strike an ironic note.*
[PHOTO: FR. BROWNE S. J.]

Opinion cartoon. One train took three hours to travel the seven miles from Dun Laoghaire to Dublin, the passengers collecting timber to feed the engine. A train from Dublin to Athlone was twice overtaken by a sailing barge on the Royal Canal. The small Irish merchant marine continued to operate, ships sailing with EIRE painted on their sides and illuminated by night. Nevertheless, 16 ships were sunk during the war, most on the Dublin–Lisbon–Dublin run. The mail boats from Holyhead were painted grey and had 13-pounder guns on the foredeck. Aer Lingus operated just a single week-day flight to Liverpool; but Foynes on the Shannon estuary quickly became an immensely busy flying-boat junction – the first stop from America – handling more than 1,400 Allied aircraft and 15,000 passengers in the one year of 1942–43.

Ireland would have been hard pushed to defend itself had any invasion taken place. Its airforce was limited to not much more than Lysander observation craft and a handful of Gloster Gladiators, plus Avro-Ansons and Walrus Amphibians; during the war it was forced to repair several Allied aircraft, which had crash-landed in Ireland, in order to raise its numbers. The Navy had some motor torpedo boats and two patrol vessels.

The Army itself was larger, of course, but inevitably suffered shortages of weapons and equipment – it had barely 20 armoured cars and no tanks. Some of the armoured cars constructed by blacksmiths in Carlow using Ford chassis, became known, perhaps inevitably, as the 'Carlow Panzers'. An example of what might have happened to the south occurred in April and May 1941, when Belfast was hit by major bombing raids. The city was ill-prepared – presumably on the assumption Northern Ireland was inconveniently far for German bombers – and the devastation was tremendous. Over 1,000 people were killed (900 in one night) and, as the toll mounted, bodies overflowed the morgues, some having to be laid out in the Falls Road baths and, as the coffins ran out, in the empty swimming-pool itself. De Valera sent southern fire brigades to help, clearly breaking his cherished neutrality regulations, but to use his own words, 'they are our own people'. Dublin itself was bombed a few times by accident, a landmine doing the most damage in June 1941, killing thirty-two.

In the south Army intelligence was well run (again breaking Ireland's neutral status by regular reports to the Allies) and the authorities managed to round up German agents with compar-

War within war. *It is 1939, hostilities with Hitler have broken out, and yet here is an Irish demonstration in Trafalgar Square (right) protesting at the imprisonment of IRA members (including the young Brendan Behan) in England and Ireland. As recently as 25 August, one of their bombs, left in a bicycle basket, had killed five in the main street of Coventry.*

Hot news. *A crowd reads the latest edition of the* Cork Independent *(left), displayed in the newspaper's office window, in 1939.*
[PHOTO: FR. BROWNE S. J.]

atively little trouble. The Germans themselves did not help matters by landing a bizarre assortment of spies, including two South Africans and an Indian near Baltimore in 1940. The latter strode off down a country road wearing a bright silk Indian suit and a straw hat, and was quickly arrested, as were the other two. (The police reported to Army intelligence that 'two whites and a nigger have appeared from nowhere'.) Irishmen who were parachuted back home by the Abwehr either regarded this as an opportunity for a cheap return flight, happily reporting to the authorities on arrival, or else made the mistake of confiding in the wrong people: one man returned to his Clare home where his father handed him to the police and collected the £500 reward, which he considerately invested for his son.

Contact was made between elements of the IRA and German agents but the two sides were dismayed with each other. The IRA was at war not only with the British but the Dublin government. They had broken with de Valera in the 1930s, being branded as illegal in 1936. After that date and during the war the government did not shirk from draconian measures: hundreds were interned without trial, six IRA men executed, and another three hunger strikers left to starve to

death. They represented the extreme edge of the nationalist force which might have been aroused had de Valera abandoned neutrality and come in with Britain.

Churchill never really grasped these pressures on de Valera; like many unregenerate imperialists he also found it hard to understand how any country could want to leave the British Empire. In his victory address of 1945 he took the opportunity to jeer at Ireland's neutral status; which in turn allowed de Valera to make one of his best speeches. The tone he adopted was measured and statesmanlike, enabling him to produce a conclusion which went straight to the hearts of his wireless audience: 'Mr Churchill is proud of Britain's stand alone, after France had fallen, and before America had entered the war. Could he not find in his heart the generosity to acknowledge that there is a small nation that stood alone, not for one year or two, but for several hundred years, against aggression; that endured spoliations, famines, massacres in endless succession; that was clubbed many times into insensibility but each time, on returning to consciousness, took up the fight anew; a small nation that could never be got to accept defeat and has never surrendered her soul?'

Nevertheless, Ireland did find itself in the diplomatic wilder-

ness following the Second World War. Until 1956 the country was excluded from the UN by the Soviet Union's veto, which argued that because Ireland had been neutral it was not a 'peace-loving nation'. But most in Ireland were unembarrassed by world condemnation, and in any case could point out that only Britain itself and France could pull moral rank since they were the two countries to have entered the war voluntarily. If Ireland had been attacked it would have fought too. One strange example of Ireland's remoteness from the anti-Nazi struggle lingered on until the early 1970s: the firm 'Swastika Laundry' whose smart vans emblazoned with an enormous red swastika on a white background (and the self justifying legend 'est. 1912') roamed Dublin's streets. One had nearly run over

Heinrich Boll in 1954, giving the ex-German soldier a frightful scare.

At the first post-war elections in 1948, Fianna Fail was by far the largest single party, but it did not have an overall majority in the Dail. To some surprise, Fine Gael managed to put together a coalition with the minority parties, and John Costello now became Taoiseach. There was little change on the social and economic front, the country remaining deep in the grip of material poverty and far from the post-war boom beginning in Europe. In political matters the new government – urged on by the most dynamic minister, Sean McBride, leader of Clann na Poblachta, a small independent party, and despite Fine Gael's ancestry as the pro-Treaty party – took the final nationalist step by declaring Ireland to be a Republic, inaugurated on Easter Monday 1949. Sinn Fein and the IRA, of course, refused to recognise this truncated Republic of Ireland – but to many the IRA by that time seemed a spent force.

Through the 1950s the Fine Gael coalition and Fianna Fail exchanged power. The first Fine Gael coalition lasted until 1951; then Fianna Fail ruled until 1954 and its replacement by the coalition; finally in 1957 Fianna Fail returned with a large majority. The great man remained Taoiseach until 1959 when he was elected President to serve two full terms before retirement in 1973. In this last stage of his life de Valera had become the nation's father figure. Much of Ireland's 20th-century history was bound up in his tall, impressive shape, even if it was, as one critic alleged, 'the case of a Rolls-Royce chassis and a Ford engine'. He looked the perfect statesman: tall, ascetic, remote, half blind, and with great natural dignity. At funerals he made a splendid figure, ramrod straight in the pouring rain. His vision of Ireland had not really altered from his earliest days: a 32-county Irish-speaking nation, whose countryside (as he said in a wireless broadcast in 1943) 'would be bright with cosy homesteads … the romping of sturdy chil-

dren, the contests of athletic youths and laughter of comely maidens, whose firesides would be forums for the wisdom of serene old age.' It is customary now to poke fun at such an arcadian vision; but he spoke for many and, with courage and determination, went some way to achieve his ideal.

Somebody once remarked that de Valera was the genius who took the socialism out of Irish republicanism. While perhaps true, there has never been much socialism in Ireland to remove in the first place. Until recently Ireland was the only European country not to possess a sizeable left-wing party with some commitment, however weak, towards public ownership or even economic planning. So Ireland in the 1950s and for most of the 1960s remained unreformed and hostile to progress. What changed it was largely the adoption of new economic ideas – in effect Keynesian borrowing – but also a shift towards the wider world, best demonstrated by its vigorous role in the United Nations. Two Irishmen made their mark in this forum in the late 1950s and early 1960s, Frederick Boland and Conor Cruise O'Brien, while Irish troops fought, and died, in various theatres, most noticeably the Congo.

The economic take-off in the 1960s, which after some hic-

Honouring the dead.

Remembrance Sunday, Limerick, c. 1955. Two men wear First World War medals (left) while the man in the second row, with the wreath in the shape of the RAF insignia, wears medals from the Second World War. The participation of large numbers from the south in the Second World War still stirs controversy, as does the wearing of poppies. A lorry (right) carries bodies of Irish soldiers, flown back from the Congo where they had been killed while serving with United Nations forces in the early 1960s. This international organisation, like the European Community, paradoxically has been used by Ireland to bolster its own national identity. They both act as counterweights against the pull of Great Britain.

Grace Kelly, *by now Princess Grace of Monaco, visits the village (left) where her people lived before they emigrated to the USA in the 19th century.*

President Kennedy *(above) at the former Viceregal Lodge in Phoenix Park, Dublin, in 1963, shortly before his assassination. It has never done an American politician any harm to play the Irish card.*

Vision and reality. *The great man, de Valera (above), liked to celebrate family values and the happy gatherings of children (above). His vision was of 'the romping of sturdy children', but the scene on the feast of Corpus Christi in Dublin in 1969 qualifies his words somewhat. Children (left) seem to swarm rather than romp and the beautiful Georgian houses are going to rack and ruin. He left work still to be done.*
[PHOTO, LEFT: ELINOR WILTSHIRE]

coughs has broadly continued, bringing Ireland's per capita income very close to Britain's, is usually attributed to a civil servant, T. K. Whitaker, and the Taoiseach who replaced de Valera – Sean Lemass. After 1973 the European Union also has added its not inconsiderable share. The ending of Ireland's forty years in the social and economic wilderness can be symbolised by a host of innovations and changes. Irish dogs had attacked the odd passing car in the 1950s, but they now, in the 1960s, lazily watched motorised prosperity pass their doors. The writer, Colm Tobin, however, believes the defining moment arrived when yogurt became available for the first time in Enniscorthy in 1972.

CHAPTER SEVEN

NORTHERN IRELAND
1920-72

Lift off. *Shorts flying boats, made in Belfast, were at the cutting edge of civil aviation in the 1930s, and their Sunderlands were a vital element in anti-submarine warfare in the 1940s. Shorts, along with Harland and Wolff the shipbuilders, represented something unique to the north, a level of technical and industrial activity which the south could not begin to rival.*

IMAGINE A COUNTRY WHERE EVERY YEAR THE majority of the inhabitants celebrate a holiday either by taking part in massive marches, or else enthusiastically witnessing the same. Although this is the height of summer (12 July) many men are clasping tightly rolled umbrellas, wearing dark suits, little bowler hats – hardly glimpsed in the City of London since the 1950s – white gloves, and, most important of all, an orange sash around their necks. An enormous noise can be heard from literally hundreds of bands, each beating out a marching rhythm. Suppose if you would the marchers divided into Lodges, each with a gigantic banner, carried aloft as if a holy sail, and bearing impassioned inscriptions such as 'Save the Covenant' and 'If God be with us who can be against us?' Then let it be explained to the curious bystander that all this is happening in a part of the United Kingdom, and is in fact a commemoration by the protestants of that region of a victory by one English king (born a Dutchman) over another, newly deposed, English king at an obscure river in Ireland in 1690. One way to judge this annual event is to look at it genially as Europe's greatest folk-festival; the other, as the Orange Order's reminder to the catholics of Northern Ireland that the protestants are the ones with the power, and they intend to keep it that way. Even with this explanation the outsider can still be mystified by all the 17th-century paraphernalia. One English visitor, upon enquiring who was this King Billy and the Boyne and the Twelfth the Orangemen were celebrating, was curtly informed 'Och away home and read your Bible, man!' Marches marking the 12th of July have been taking place in Northern Ireland since the early 19th century at least. Lady Pamela Campbell was the wife of a British general stationed in Armagh in 1828, a place she called 'the positive pips of the orange'. She recorded that 'we shall, it is hardly doubted, have a row here, for our Orangemen are frantic, and *will* walk and *will* play their horrid tunes.' There is every sign of these rites continuing well into the 21st century.

As with so many partitions around the world, few imagined Ireland's would be permanent. The Government of Ireland Act of 1920, which by offering two parliaments in effect divided the island, also made provision for a Council of Ireland overarching both northern and southern parliaments. The theory was that representatives would be elected from each assembly with gradually accumulating powers, moving towards 'the eventual establishment of a parliament for the whole of Ireland'. Such a conclusion remained (and remains) an aspira-

Stormont. *Northern Ireland's parliament building (left) surrenders its park to grow food for the war effort. Ulster became a key centre of wartime production. The buildings destroyed and the lives lost in the* Belfast Blitz *were further testimony to the strength of their cause in the eyes of Unionists. More than 1,000 were killed in April and May 1941, partly because Belfast had never expected to be raided.*

Derry harbour *in 1944 (above), full of Royal and US Navy destroyers involved in North Atlantic convoy duties. Its strategic position in relation to the Western Approaches made it a priceless asset in the war against the German U boats.*

tion, however, and as far as the northern unionists were concerned their job was to extract as much as they could from a home rule parliament which they had not desired. It did not take long before they began to realise that a devolved assembly could be turned into an anchor for the union and their own position.

The North of Ireland parliament, in charge of internal affairs, comprised a House of Commons of fifty-two members and Senate of twenty-six – the latter with minimal powers. The whole was housed at Stormont, a huge classical pile, especially built to emphasise the solemnity of this legislative body, and carefully sited at the end of an imposing avenue dominated by a statue of Carson. To one side stood an even more incongruous building, the mock-medieval castle which housed the Cabinet Office of the Northern Ireland Prime Minister and his ministers. They formed the executive which ran the north, apart from foreign affairs and related matters still handled by the imperial parliament. In view of these retained powers, Northern Ireland continued to have thirteen MPs at Westminster.

The Unionist party proceeded to form the first government in Northern Ireland – and then remained in power uninterruptedly for the next fifty years, a tenure surpassed only by the Communist party in the old USSR. This was not surprising, since the raison d'etre for Northern Ireland was its inbuilt unionist majority. That was why the new unit comprised just six counties from the nine-county province of Ulster – the maximum territory which could be controlled by the protestants. It was the size of the protestant majority in the population which guaranteed the safety of unionism. Elections ran along well grooved lines. Floating voters between the unionist majority and nationalist minority simply did not exist. Many Unionist seats were uncontested, such was the foregone conclusion.

Because the Unionist party included virtually all the protestants in the north it spanned the range of social classes. Until the 1970s its leaders were drawn from the intertwined gentry class. Northern Ireland's fourth and fifth Prime Ministers, for example, Captain Terence O'Neill and Major James Chichester-Clarke, were cousins, the sons (and in Chichester-Clarke's case grandson too) of MPs; old Etonians, ex Irish Guards officers, replete with upper-class voices and mannerisms. Both had served in the Second World War (two of O'Neill's brothers being killed) and, as was the custom in the north, clung to their military titles. Earlier, Northern Ireland had been led by two stalwarts of similar hue, who were at the helm for nearly forty years – James Craig, later Lord Craigavon, and Basil Brooke, later Lord Brookeborough. On the domestic political front, in effect nothing moved from 1921 to 1968. The glue which united these gentlemen and the protestant rank and file was the Orange Order, membership of which was vital for political advancement or the enjoyment of patronage. It was Craig who best summarised the connection: 'I have always said that I am an Orangeman first and politician afterwards; all I boast is that we are a Protestant Parliament for a Protestant State.'

What of those who were not protestants but living in this 'Protestant State'? Roughly one third of the population were catholic and overwhelmingly nationalist. At first their leaders ignored the Northern Irish parliament, banking on the Boundary Commission to so weaken the north that union with Dublin would be unavoidable. When this hope proved false, after 1925, they entered Stormont in order to better their position, but did not agree to become the official opposition until the 1960s. Brian Moore's early novels of Belfast catholics, both middle and working class, sharply illustrate the minority's uncompromising ghetto attitude. It was this reluctance of the minority, the fact that it did not form a 'loyal' opposition, as it were, and refused to accept the legitimacy of the northern state, which encouraged the unionists' well-documented seige mentality.

Broadly expressed, unionists believed their duty was to protect the British heritage in north-east Ireland and that had to mean no concessions to the catholic minority. For though a majority in Northern Ireland, the unionists were, of course, a minority in Ireland as a whole. Should they let slip their vigilance, and allow catholic nationalists power in whatever sphere, then the state could be threatened. Hence the emotive slogans from the 17th century and later: No Surrender!; Not an Inch!; Ulster is British!; No Pope Here! (Spotted on a wall in Belfast

A big ship *near completion at Harland and Wolff in 1954 (left). Their last really big liner, the* Canberra *was launched in 1960, beginning a long career cruising or carrying emigrants (many Irish) to Australia before being pressed into service during the Falklands War.*

The Comet, *the world's first jet airliner, being built at Short Brothers in Belfast (right), keeping Britain at the forefront of technology – and in debt to Ulster.*

in 1976, that last cry had an additional graffito below it: 'Lucky Old Pope'.) It was assumed, with some justification, that most catholics were nationalists; and also, with less justification, that none of them could be trusted with positions of responsibility. Hence the discrimination against the minority. In part this came about from a genuine dislike and fear of catholicism from the northern protestants, many of them Presbyterians and traditionally hostile to Romish customs. A BBC interviewer in 1970: 'What do you have against Roman Catholics?' Belfast protestant: 'Are you daft? Why their religion, of course.' But the usual line was that the catholics were constitutionally disloyal and hence traitors to the state. 'Catholics were out to destroy Ulster with all their might and power', said Sir Basil Brooke in 1933. He went on to advise giving employment only to protestants. 'I feel I can speak freely on this subject as I have not had a Roman Catholic about my own place … I would appeal to loyalists therefore, wherever possible, to employ good protestant lads and lassies.'

Discrimination undoubtedly operated, but in a far more mild and covert way than racial legislation in other countries. Comparisons with apartheid are inappropriate. Many catholics, however, did find themselves disadvantaged at a local level. Northern Ireland had been established with proportional representation as the voting system specifically to protect minority interests; but the Unionist government managed to get rid of PR for both provincial and local elections. A large number of catholics did not have a vote at local elections since the franchise extended only to property owners or tenants of council houses, and their spouses. Being the poorest section of the community, this hit the catholics more than the protestants. Hence the crucial issue of housing allocation. As Austin Currie, one of the Civil Rights leaders in the late 1960s, put it: 'The allocation of a public authority house was not just the allocation of a house. It was the allocation of two votes. Therefore, in marginal areas, he who controlled the allocation of public authority housing effectively controlled the voting in that area.' Thus it could happen that an area with a catholic majority could have a protestant council – which in turn would keep the status quo by favouring protestants when it came to housing.

Gerrymandering also came into play to guarantee inbuilt protestant majorities. The most splendid example was Londonderry City Council where 14,000 catholic voters ended up with eight councillors from one large ward, and 9,000

protestant voters enjoyed twelve councillors from two nicely calculated, wards. No surprise then that housing and jobs tended to go to the protestants. Some spectacularly naked gerrymandering occurred at Armagh where the city boundary, following the line of a certain terrace, suddenly leapt behind the back-gardens of three, blemishing, catholic houses. Conor Cruise O'Brien recounts how an English Jesuit on a fact-finding tour in the early 1950s remarked 'How perfectly stupid!' to his guide, a nationalist politician, when shown this careful alteration. 'In the name of God', said the politician with true northern rigour, 'what's *stupid* about it?' Besides some local government jobs, catholics quickly learnt there was little point in applying for work with some private businesses, even giant concerns such as Short Brothers, the aircraft manufacturers, or Harland and Wolff, the Belfast shipbuilders. Those who did get posts found promotion hard or impossible. Denis Donoghue writes about his father, a sergeant in the RUC between the wars, who could not be promoted: 'He was not a Protestant, therefore he was not a Unionist, therefore he was not a member of the Loyal Order of Orangemen, therefore … '

Donoghue also claims that, as a boy living in Warrenpoint in Northern Ireland, he was able to spot a protestant at a hundred yards. 'In the North a Protestant walks with an air of possession and authority, regardless of his social class. He walks as if he owns the place, which indeed he does.' Others were less

The marching season. *Two members of the Orange Order have doffed their bowlers and laid aside their umbrellas while they have lunch (left). Their fringed sashes indicate to which lodge of the Order they belong. Orange parades used to be tolerated by most catholics, even enjoyed as something to brighten the often dull Ulster summers. But after 1970 they became unloved symbols of oppression. The fierce tribal rhythms beaten out on drums with the squeal of fifes rising above them is the music to which the marchers step out. Three generations of the same family show off their Lambeg drums in Ballymena in the early 1980s (above): 'It is the drums pre-side, like giant tumours.'*
[PHOTO, ABOVE: BOBBY HANVEY]
[PHOTO, LEFT: KLAUS FRANCKE]

sharp eyed, but identification in this sectarian world could be crucial for further prospects. Clues depended on names, addresses, most of all on schools attended. One nationalist remembered that in the 1960s 'when I applied for a job, my father, who wasn't political anyway, told us not to put "Falls Road" as our address. We would put "Broadway" which is a pretty neutral area close by. Our name, Gorman, was near enough neutral as well. We weren't O'Shaughnessy or Murphy.' Surnames could be deceptive, however – Murphy was the name of the leader of the protestant Shankill Butchers, a group of thugs convicted of torturing and killing catholics. That Murphy's first name was Lennie, though, and Leonard was an exclusively protestant christian name in the north. Seamus Heaney has summed it all up:

Smoke-signals are loud-mouthed compared with us:
Manoeuvrings to find out name and school,
Subtle discrimination by addresses
With hardly an exception to the rule

That Norman, Ken and Sidney signalled Prod
And Seamus (call me Sean) was sure-fire Pape.
O land of password, handgrip, wink and nod,
Of open minds as open as a trap,...

A host of stories, some perhaps not apocryphal, have been told to illustrate the implacable confessional divide. The Orange Order in Agohill, County Antrim, was considered

utterly copper-bottomed in bigotry, yet one of their members turned Papist on his deathbed. Consternation and bewilderment; but it turned out he had done the deed in order to rid the world of a Taig instead of a true prot. Then an English colonel who had retired to Northern Ireland had put agnostic on his census return. 'No problem, no problem at all', said the local official, 'but would that be a protestant agnostic or a catholic agnostic?' Once an Ulster newspaper headline was supposed to have read: 'Protestants and Catholics united in their hatred of Ecumenicism.'

Throughout the north the two communities lived their separate lives; but for the minority there was little to chuckle over in the situation. Control lay with the unionists; in literal terms with the Special Powers Act of 1922, which allowed the government emergency powers to search, arrest and detain without warrant. The bill was described at its passing as unnecessarily long by a vexed nationalist, since one sentence would have been sufficient: 'The home secretary shall have power to do whatever he likes.' Catholics felt the act was applied far too rigorously against their people; the government could point out the continual constitutional threat from nationalists, and moreover occasional IRA attacks, as during its abortive 'campaign' from 1956 to 1962. Catholics also resented the largely protestant police force (the RUC); the government, with some justification, claimed that comparatively few catholics volunteered.

But real contempt and fear were reserved by the catholics for the B Specials – a reserve police body, exclusively protestant and aggressively Orange. For the minority the catchphrase was Law and Orange Order.

That Northern Ireland was unlike normal democracies few would deny; though the blame for this governing without consensus, as a sociologist would label it, varied according to each commentator's sympathies. What is clear enough is that British governments at Whitehall, whether Conservative or Labour, did nothing to force any reform in the north. The line was to ignore any internal matters as being under the remit of Stormont. The Tories may have enjoyed the votes of the Ulster Unionists and seen no reason to rock the boat; yet even Labour averted its gaze. James Callaghan, Home Secretary when the balloon went up in the late 1960s, later confessed that 'yes, theoretically and logically, we should have taken action to press the Stormont government to do things'; but that 'like so many things in politics it took a crisis to enable us to take the action that was necessary'. There was also the case that discrimination against the minority never sparked a dramatic event to catch the world's attention – for instance, no Sharpeville-type massacre as in South Africa. Repression there was, but it was largely sapping, low-profile intimidation, with no horrors to alert outside interest. And for many of the protestant working class there was little sense that they formed part of a privileged group. 'As a boy on the Shankill Road', said one, 'if I was a "first class citizen", I never knew it. I ran around with me arse out of me trousers, just like the bloody Taigs.'

In the 1960s a number of factors came together to force change on the ruling structure represented by the Unionists at Stormont. Strangely enough, one of the agents of change came from within the smooth face of Unionist rule itself: the appointment of Terence O'Neill as Prime Minister of Northern Ireland in 1963. O'Neill understood the need for better relations with the catholic minority, and he proceeded, gently, to probe for cracks in the reactionary nature of unionist rule. He

Bad omen. *A boy anticipates the violence to come with his toy guns, as a civil rights march goes by, watched by relaxed RUC men in 1968 (left).*

Chalk and cheese. *William Craig (far right), a typical hard-faced Unionist, addresses the faithful*

outside Belfast City Hall in May 1972. Bernadette Devlin protests in Downing Street in 1970 (below). Fresh out of university and the youngest MP in the House of Commons, representing the nationalist camp, she was God's gift to the media. Once again the Irish Question had come back to haunt Westminster.

appointed liberal advisers, was photographed visiting a convent and smiling to nuns, made conciliatory speeches greatly different from those of his jurassic age predecessor, Lord Brookeborough, and, above all, visited and received the Republic's Prime Minister, the equally modernising Sean Lemass. But O'Neill had to be cautious. At his back were the hardfaced men of his Cabinet, such as William Craig and the ambitious Brian Faulkner, both from different backgrounds to the traditional gentry class of Unionist leaders. So too was another figure, who would achieve great prominence in the 1960s and for the next thirty years or more – the Reverend Dr Ian Paisley. The Big Man from Ballymena enjoyed two roles: the first as a fundamentalist evangelist in the classic style with constant appeals to the Bible; the second as the leader of hardcore loyalism. He encapsulates two important elements of northern protestantism – conditional loyalty and anti-catholicism. Throughout the 1960s he was active in holding marches and demonstrations against any reform or threat to his conception of protestantism. Although the government occasionally took resolute action against him – once imprisoning him for three months in 1966 (when he emerged from gaol he was

driven off in a car bearing the sign 'Behold the Lamb of God') – support grew for him, and his oratory and example were to play a key part in the riots of 1968 and 1969.

Another factor for change was the growth of a catholic middle class, or at least those who had taken advantage of the educational opportunities since the Butler Act of 1944. Many who were at university in the 1960s looked about them and instead of treating discrimination simply as the way things were, as their parents might have done, determined to alter matters. In this they were encouraged by the mood amongst young people in the West during that decade, especially the Civil Rights campaign in America. That example had proved that peaceful agitation, protest marches, civil disobedience and the like could destroy an old repressive system. Suddenly

unionist policies which in previous decades might have been swallowed – such as starving the province west of the river Bann of funds, siting the new university not in catholic Derry where a popular college already existed, but protestant Coleraine, placing the first new city in the favoured (and protestant) east of the province and then dubbing it Craigavon – were no longer accepted with resignation by the minority.

The first sign of organisation was the formation of the Northern Ireland Civil Rights Association (NICRA) in 1967, which pushed for a number of reforms especially over the housing issue. One of its supporters, the MP Austin Currie, joined a squat in the summer of 1968 protesting against the award of a house to an 18-year-old protestant secretary of a local Unionist when hundreds of catholic families were waiting

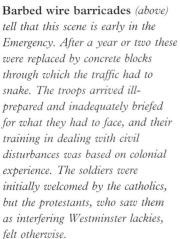

Barbed wire barricades *(above)*
tell that this scene is early in the
Emergency. After a year or two these
were replaced by concrete blocks
through which the traffic had to
snake. The troops arrived ill-
prepared and inadequately briefed
for what they had to face, and their
training in dealing with civil
disturbances was based on colonial
experience. The soldiers were
initially welcomed by the catholics,
but the protestants, who saw them
as interfering Westminster lackies,
felt otherwise.

The Bible and the bayonet *were*
neither much use in keeping the
peace. Troops were deployed to try
and stop the violence on the streets
of Londonderry, in the Bogside, in
August 1969 for the first time
(above). The soldiers desperately
tried to get between the two commu-
nities, not knowing where one began
and the other ended. In spite of the
warning from the Book of Jeremiah
sported by this protestant (left),
winter went on a long time. In the
face of IRA snipers with Armalite
rifles, the soldiers soon put away
their bayonets.

patiently. This came to be seen as the first open action of the civil rights movement. An offshoot of this movement, People's Democracy (PD), worked not only for the abolition of abuses but the introduction of general socialist measures throughout all Ireland. Irish unity itself was almost an afterthought. Prominent amongst this faction were Eamonn McCann and Bernadette Devlin, both in their twenties. Any republican element in these civil rights movements tended to be minimal, although the participants were overwhelmingly from the catholic nationalist community. The songs were 'We Shall Overcome' and the 'International', instead of the traditional republican ballads. The IRA in the north had not regained its confidence after the last campaign ended in 1962, while in the south many republicans were toying with advanced socialist ideas to the detriment of the nationalist ideal. To many unionists, however, the NICRA did appear to be a front for republicanism and therefore a threat to be resisted.

Most accounts of the current troubles in Northern Ireland start with the riots in Derry in October 1968, when a civil rights march, banned by Stormont, was broken up by the police using truncheons and water cannon. The scenes were pictured on television, and people in Britain and around the world began to discover the strange anomaly that was this part of the United Kingdom. Early in 1969 a Paisleyite mob repeatedly attacked a PD march, most spectacularly at Burntollet Bridge: 'From the lanes', writes Bernadette Devlin, one of the march's leaders, 'burst hordes of screaming people wielding planks of wood, bottles, laths, iron bars, crowbars, cudgels studded with nails, and they waded into the march beating hell out of everybody.' The attitude of the police to this attack appeared, by and large, to be indifferent. As tension increased, O'Neill sacked his reactionary Home Office Minister William Craig, and made moving appeals on television for calm between the communities; but the two sides continued to polarise. Support in the Unionist party withered for O'Neill and his attempts at reform, and in April 1969 he resigned as Prime Minister to be replaced by Major James Chichester-Clarke, promptly christened Chi Chi after a panda then in London Zoo. Paisley greeted the change with the boast (not idle) that he had brought down a captain and could bring

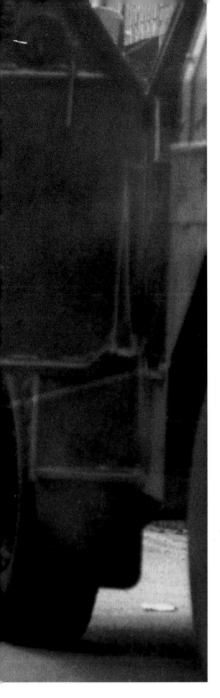

The bereaved. *A family mourns the dead (right) after Bloody Sunday. 1972, with its 470 dead, was the nadir, one hopes, of the present Troubles. Bloody Sunday certainly brought about the suspension of Stormont and its replacement by direct rule from Westminster.*
[PHOTO: GILLES PERESS]

Bloody Sunday, *January 1972, and The Parachute Regiment hand it to the IRA recruiters on a plate. Fourteen dead was the result of their loss of discipline, provoked but not excused by stone throwing and a shot or shots. Dead, dying or badly wounded, a man is carried away (left) as Fr. (now Bishop) Edward Daly waves his handkerchief in a desperate gesture to halt further shooting, while soldiers look wildly about them.*

down a major as well. In August 1969 the province erupted. The Derry Apprentice Boys' march in August celebrates protestant triumphs in the 17th century and had often led to rioting in the past. This time the police chased stone-throwing catholic youths into the Bogside, the strongly catholic area of Derry, to be met by an organised barrage of stones and petrol bombs. Tear gas was used which discomforted many, but appeared to have no effect on Bernadette Devlin, since April an MP at Westminster, who told people that 'it's OK once you get a taste of it', while she galvanised the Bogsiders and helped prepare missiles. No guns were used on either side, but the battle raged on for days, the situation not helped, first by an announcement by Jack Lynch, the Republic's Prime Minister, that the south could not stand by, which seemed to suggest to loyalists that an invasion was imminent; then the decision by Stormont to send in the detested B Specials. In Belfast the rioting was even more virulent and this time guns were used on both sides, the RUC occasionally spraying buildings with machine-gun fire from their armoured cars, while a protestant mob, including the Specials, destroyed and burnt about 200 catholic houses. (Five catholics and two protestants died; countless were wounded.) Both at Stormont and Westminster it was realised that the time had come to send in the British Army. The nationalist MP Gerry Fitt remembers ringing Jim Callaghan, the Home Secretary, and pleading with him to issue the order. 'I'll never forget his reply. "Gerry", he says, "I can get the army in but it's going to be a devil of a job to get it out."'

The British Army was welcomed by the catholics of Belfast and Derry as saviours – which was clearly the case in that

Paramilitary fashion. *A bit of posturing for the press by women members of the Official IRA ('Stickies') at an Easter parade commemorating the 1916 Rising, in Downpatrick during the early 1970s (left). Each woman wears a 'sticky' bearing the image of the Easter lily.*

Welcome home *for veteran Republican Frank McGlade (right), rounded up in the inept internment dragnet in 1971, and then released in April 1972 by the authorities after they realised that they had scored another own-goal.*
[PHOTO, LEFT: BOBBY HANVEY]

month of 1969. 'I felt like a knight in shining armour', recalls one soldier, 'it was marvellous … Tea? There was too much tea – and buns and sandwiches. They'd be out there with trays. I must have put on about a stone. The reception was fantastic.' Now that the full weight of the British government was focused on the north, commissions were appointed to investigate the causes of these riots. The Cameron Report, published in September 1969, did make some criticisms of the PD leaders, but reserved its harshest words to endorse catholic grievances over housing, gerrymandering, the absence of one man one vote and the Special Powers Act. That was bad enough for unionists to swallow; but worse was the Hunt Report the next month which recommended a thoroughgoing reform of the police and abolition of the B Specials. The reaction was heavy rioting in the Shankill Road of Belfast. A protestant sniper shot and killed a policeman – the first RUC casualty of the present troubles – while the British Army faced the loyalist mob; twenty-two soldiers were wounded, but at least two of their attackers were shot dead. Over the next few months the British forced through the reforms recommended by Cameron and Hunt – in effect almost everything for which the civil rights movement had been agitating. One exception was the abolition of Stormont itself; and it was the continuation of this government and its executive force which was one of the reasons why the catholic community gradually reversed its attitude and began to look on the British Army and security forces as the aggressors. It has been said by many commentators (some with the advantage of hindsight) that, had Westminster abolished Stormont in 1969 and taken over the running of the province, applying reform and keeping the security forces under their control, the situation might have been contained.

Irish republicans had been appalled by the events of 1969 and the welcome afforded by catholic nationalists to the ancient enemy, the British Army. That was not how the script was supposed to run. The part played by the IRA in the defence of Derry and Belfast had been practically non-existent, itself unsurprising since the personnel were few and they had virtually no weapons. Scrawled on the walls in the catholic ghettos appeared the derisive graffiti 'IRA – I Ran Away'. It was in response to this crisis that the IRA split into two in 1970. The Official IRA, moving to the Left, proposed entering constitutional politics through Sinn Fein; the more traditional wing, calling themselves the Provisionals, rejected any Marxist talk of social revolution and sought to concentrate on the simple struggle to force the British out of Northern Ireland and reunite the country. It was a time of realignment for the constitutional politicians as well. The Unionist monolith split in 1971 with Ian Paisley leading the more extreme faction into his custom-built Democratic Unionist Party (DUP), leaving behind the Official or Ulster Unionist Party, from March 1971 under Brian Faulkner, Prime Minister after Chichester-Clarke had resigned. Nationalists under the leadership of Gerry Fitt, John Hume and Austin Currie formed the Social Democratic Labour Party (SDLP) in August 1970. That year also saw the British General Election with the Tories replacing Labour. The Home Secretary now responsible for Northern Ireland became Reginald Maudling, whose relaxed attitude contrasted with the energy of Callaghan. Maudling's contribution is best demonstrated by his celebrated remark on the flight home after his first visit to the province. 'For God's sake, bring me a large Scotch. What a bloody awful country!'

Confrontation slowly approached between the British Army and the Provisionals. In July 1970 the Army conducted an arms raid on the Falls Road which led to a riot and eventual gun battle. During the process many homes were wrecked and five civilians killed; weapons indeed were found but the Belfast nationalists began to turn towards the IRA as their protectors. The Army was seen as acting on behalf of Stormont and its sectarian interests. The first killing of a British soldier did not occur until February 1971, but thereafter the pace was fast and furious: in that year the Provisionals went on to shoot dead another 41 soldiers; the next year 64, most of them by snipers. In August 1971 Faulkner persuaded a reluctant British government and sceptical Army that internment was the answer. Unfortunately the move was counter-productive since only republican suspects were arrested, and of these 300, few were genuine or current IRA men. Most of the actual Provisional

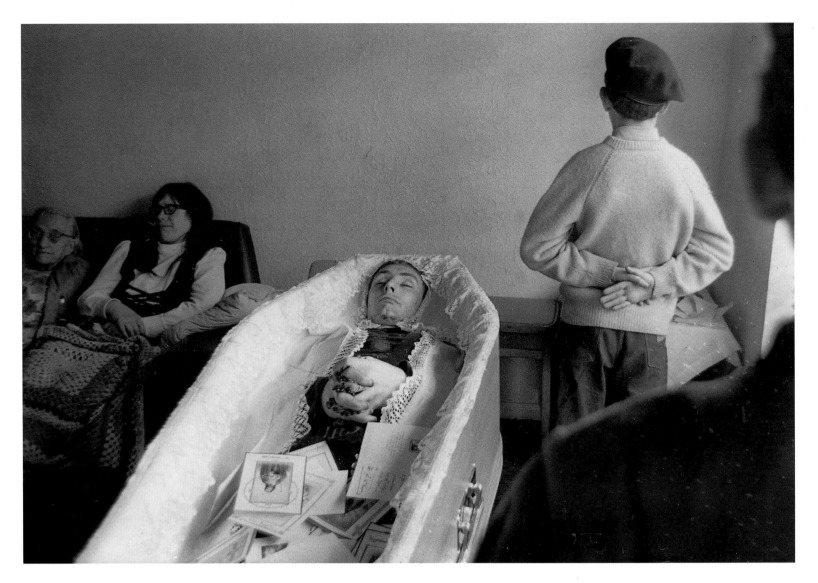

leaders had gone on the run; instead one Army officer remembers an elderly man well into his eighties 'who was rather proud to be arrested. He said "I'm delighted to think that I'm still a trouble to the British government but I have to tell you I have not been active since the Easter rising."' Many who were arrested were ill treated, and when released proved enthusiastic recruits to the IRA. Early in 1972 came the incident which led, finally, to the abolition of the Unionist government in Northern Ireland. For many months there had been rioting in Derry, with soldiers being pelted daily by stone throwers – traditionally round about tea time after school ended. An anti-internment march had been called for – though Stormont had made all marches illegal – and when the inevitable stone throwing started paratroopers rushed forward and shot dead fourteen civilians. It remains a highly controversial episode, but most now accept that the Army had been fired upon fifteen minutes earlier that day (even if it had been only one shot); and that, despite Lord Widgery's subsequent findings, none of those killed had been carrying any offensive weapons.

Bloody Sunday, as it was rapidly dubbed by the press, proved another recruiting incentive for the IRA. More killings, including by car bombs, were conducted by the Provisionals. Loyalist forces added to the mayhem and murder. The

Lost youth. *A young boy wearing an IRA beret stands guard by the open coffin of Joseph McGann (above), a top IRA man reputed by his own to have killed fifteen British soldiers. In 1972 he failed to stop at a checkpoint and died as he had lived. For a whole generation of children the Emergency has been their only experience of life.*

A Belfast bin warrior mimicking *the RUC and soldiers with their riot shields and batons (right). Dustbin lids like this were beaten as a warning of the police or Army's approach in the Bogside and the Falls Road.*

province seemed to be spiralling into anarchy. In March 1972 the British government announced that Stormont would be suspended and that Northern Ireland would be administered directly from Westminster under the supervision of a Secretary of State. It was widely seen, correctly, as a victory for the nationalists. At the end of her book, *The Price of My Soul*, published in 1969, Bernadette Devlin had anticipated that day: 'Now we are witnessing [the Unionist Party Government's] dying convulsions. And with traditional Irish mercy, when we've got it down we will kick it into the ground.' But the decision, as so often in the story of Britain in Ireland, proved to be too late. The powder keg was truly lit. That year in Northern Ireland 470 people were despatched in various ways – and the scene set for the next twenty years and more.

The Big Man from Ballymena.
The Rev. Ian Paisley echoes the gesture of the statue of Edward Carson outside Stormont. Inflexible foe of Popery and Republicanism, brilliant self-publicist and brutal but effective orator – he has brooded over Ulster like a black thunder cloud since the 1960s, matching the intransigence of the IRA step by step. But there are plenty of fellow-Ulstermen who need little persuading, a ready-made constituency for him and his hard line.
[PHOTO: BOBBY HANVEY]

Ethnic cleansing. *A catholic family, burnt or frightened out of their home by protestant neighbours, about to start their journey to Dublin, refugees from their birthplace. Protestants were subjected to the same treatment – there is little originality in tribal warfare. It is estimated that 60,000 were forced out of their homes between 1969 and 1972, some 80 per cent of them catholics.*

CHAPTER EIGHT

IRELAND TODAY

THE INHABITANTS OF THE REPUBLIC OF IRELAND today pursue a less straightforward policy towards Nothern Ireland than forty years ago. The national aspiration largely remains unification, but the mood is St Augustine's – 'O Lord, give us unity but not yet'; plus the majority rider of 'peaceably and with the consent of the north'. It is hard to generalise, but the mood has shifted from suspicion of Britain's role in Northern Ireland to a more amicable partnership. One of the subtle signs has been the general custom of southern politicians and administrators referring to 'Northern Ireland', instead of the 'Six Counties' which was quite common in the 1960s. The latter phrase implied an impermanent area and unfinished business. Unreconstructed republicans would even refer to the south as the Twenty-six Counties, not willing to award the sacred title of Republic to an amputated body. Northerners, both protestant and catholic, sometimes still refer today to the south as the Free State. Well-meaning foreigners, anxious to get it right, occasionally address the south as Eire – but the official title, and one now used unconcernedly by most Irishmen, is the Republic of Ireland.

The Republic today is far more of an autonomous sovereign state than when it became the Irish Free State in 1921. Not only in the obvious constitutional sense, but because over the last forty years it has developed economically and become transformed into one of the smaller, prosperous western European countries. Indeed its growth rate over the last few years has been the highest in Europe, winning the accolade of the Celtic Tiger. Over a generation it has become self-confident, modern and, above all, European. Economic historians traditionally discover the origin of this change in the Whitaker report of 1958 and the adoption of these broadly Keynesian ideas by the new Taoiseach, Sean Lemass. The State became involved in industrial planning, encouraged foreign investment, borrowed expansively; and if recently it has throttled back on some of these emphases, it is still far more *dirigiste* than is fashionable in the Anglo-American world today. In 1969 the Industrial Development Authority (IDA) was established to entice foreign companies to settle in Ireland – with much success. By the mid 1990s nearly 40 per cent of Irish industry was foreign owned, mostly American, British and German, and these new firms accounted for 70 per cent of manufactured exports. The companies came to Ireland because of generous grants and light taxation arranged by the IDA, but also because of a well-educated, comparatively low-waged workforce, which by the 1990s had achieved excellent labour relations with the employers. And, as always, the south of Ireland continued to

Allied Irish Banks HQ, *Ballsbridge, Dublin. Dublin had already witnessed modern architecture under the architect Michael Scott in the 1950s, but that had been done cheaply and at the expense of the city's Georgian heritage. Now Georgian Dublin, much of it restored and appreciated, sits alongside some of the most imaginatively and expensively built corporation buildings anywhere in Europe. A combination of Dublin's European outlook and its young city population has made it dynamic and a favourite corporate and tourist destination.*

One for the pot. *(Top) The greyhounds have been exercised – the small boys too – and an unlucky rabbit is shortly going to find its way into a stew. Behind the men is a bank, not the hedge typical of the English countryside; beyond, the rolling green fields and, mercifully, not a bungalow in sight.*

Hands are slapped *to seal the deal at Castlewellan Fair, County Down (left). The horse still looms large in the minds if not the lives of many Irishmen. Copious rain grows lush pasture which feeds healthy – and fast – bloodstock.*

Youth takes the reins (above) at Ballinasloe Horse Fair, Galway. A boy rides a piebald pony bareback, putting it through its paces for the benefit of possible buyers in the 1980s. This picture symbolises the best of old Ireland going forward briskly under the guidance of new hands. The route it has taken has been firmly into Europe, away from the land in great numbers, and out from under the skirts of the Church. Thanks to the galloping growth rate at home, young boys such as this no longer have to leave Ireland to find work, as they did in the 1950s and 1960s.

[PHOTOS, TOP LEFT AND ABOVE: KLAUS FRANCKE; BOTTOM LEFT: BOBBY HANVEY]

207

be conservative socially and thus reassuring for foreign capital.

A further reason for inward investment has been Ireland's membership of the European Union. It is hard to exaggerate the economic advantages enjoyed by Ireland since it joined up (with Britain) in 1973. At a stroke it gained access to an expensive food policy which might have been designed for an agricultural country; and later, once its industrial goods appeared, entry into the fast-growing EC market. Moreover, membership meant it could break away from economic subordination to Britain: before entry over 70 per cent of all Irish exports went to Britain; by 1987 only 34 per cent. When the EMS was created in 1979 Ireland entered straightaway, unlike Britain which joined later (and departed earlier). Its independent pound, the punt, is recognised as a stable currency; and the major political parties have supported its entry into the EMU. The Irish are extremely good Europeans, not least in knowing how to work the system to their advantage. Ireland has obtained literally billions from the Community's structural funds (between 1973 and 1991 £14 billion) and although governments generally have been reticent on the benefits obtained, at certain moments – such as over the Maastricht Treaty which required popular endorsement – it admits to the figures. In that year, 1992, Ireland enjoyed six times more than it put in. Much of the cake has come from the CAP which for many years was a licence to produce endless dairy products at fixed intervention prices. Even with the stricter regime of subsidy reform and quotas, Irish farmers are still benefitting. Indeed, the growth rate for 1997, estimated at 8 per cent, comfortably more than twice Britain's, is partly explained by the monthly cheque from Brussels which one accountant has reckoned to be 3 per cent of the Irish economy – itself a decline from 5 per cent in the early 1990s. Yet it is not just a matter of economic self-interest which has made the Irish into Europeans par excellence, but a genuine idealism for European-wide initiatives as well as desire to escape political dependence on Britain. Irish self-confidence has gained in the process, not least from its adept handling of the rotating presidency.

Modernisation has not been without its pains of course. For a country with many small farmers, the writing has been on the wall for decades, recently hastened by the EU's agricultural reforms. The move from the land to the cities increases yearly – and by cities one really means Dublin, already an astonishing million plus, almost one third of the entire Republic's population. (Can there be another country with such an enormous metropolis relative to its size?) As the countryside loses its numbers it has changed its appearance too.

The new Ireland. *Teenagers at a U2 open-air concert in Croke Park, Dublin, in 1987, raucously enjoying themselves like young people throughout the rest of Europe. It was* *rumoured that for some years the earnings of this group were second only to EC payments in their contribution to the Irish economy.*
[PHOTO: DEREK SPEIRS]

Peaks and troughs. *Pilgrims say their rosaries on the misty summit of Croagh Patrick, the holy mountain in County Mayo, during the 1980s (right). Some climb in bare feet, which are often left bloodied and* *sore from the sharp stones of the slippery, slidy terrain. The backsliding Bishop Eamon Casey (above, right) with his predecessor Bishop Michael Browne of Galway.* [PHOTO, RIGHT: KLAUS FRANCKE]

Many prosperous farmers have moved out of their cottages and into bungalows, many custom-built from the plans in a book called *Bungalow Bliss* – loftily dubbed Bungalow Blight by the Dublin intelligentsia. The countryside began to be dotted by these low white buildings, many with vaguely Moorish arches and verandahs – the Alhambra of Skibbereen, the Casbah of Ballydehob. In turn, some of the rejected cottages have been purchased and done up by holidaying Englishmen, which provides a satisfying circularity to the proceedings.

As the countryside has changed so has society, in particular the position of the Church. No longer does it enjoy that automatic deference and authority of old. On a number of issues its stance has been challenged and overturned: no longer is Ireland the only European country not to allow contraception or divorce. The change came about largely by public debate and discussion in the media. The old guard blamed television – 'there was no sex in Ireland until the BBC came' – and certainly many topics were first aired on Gay Byrne's *Late, Late Show* on RTE. On contraception, divorce and abortion, the Church has had to concede defeat or to compromise, although it fought vigorously and slowed the liberal advance. On the matter of contraception, for instance, the battle raged between the reformers, the government and the courts (with the Church a commanding presence in the background) throughout the 1960s and 1970s; until in 1979 it was ordained that contraceptives could be sold in chemists' shops to married couples, and on a doctor's prescription. The minister who piloted this bill though the Dail announced it as 'an Irish solution to an Irish problem'. It was not until the 1990s that contraception became freely available irrespective of status. Abortion remains

banned but advice on facilities in Britain is now allowed to be publicised – again after an almighty struggle. The Church's opposition to sexual liberalisation was not helped by a number of scandals in the 1990s concerning aberrant priests, the most spectacular of which was the revelation of Bishop Casey's child. Instantly T-shirts appeared throughout the country: 'Wear a condom – just in Casey.'

Although the Church might have been buffeted over the past decades, Ireland is still one of the most devout countries in Europe. Attendance at Mass is far higher than in other catholic countries such as France, Italy and Spain. Pilgrimages are undertaken to Knock, Lough Derg, Croagh Patrick; the Angelus sounds on television at six o'clock; people cross themselves passing a church. Outside many towns and villages there will be a grotto to the Virgin Mary. In 1985 the statue at Ballinspittle in County Cork was seen to move and, despite official Church disapproval, parties of the devout were soon making their way there. Credulous or not, the Irish as a whole

Committed to a greater cause.
Bob Geldof (right) formerly of the Boomtown Rats, took up the cause of starving Africa and shook the public conscience by the neck until it disgorged millions for his Live Aid charity. He is seen here with President Hillery after handing over a Live Aid cheque. His then wife, Paula Yates, stands behind him. The talents of Sinead O'Connor (left) often became submerged by her publicity grabbing actions, such as tearing up photographs of the Pope on stage. Michael Flatley (above), a Chicago-Irishman, applied the razzamatazz, scale and discipline of the Broadway routine to traditional Irish dancing in the phenomenally popular shows Riverdance *and* Lord of the Dance.
[PHOTO, TOP RIGHT: PADRAIG MACBRIAN]

practise more charity than other countries. It was Bob Geldof, of course, who inspired Live Aid, and the Irish regularly donate more aid per capita to the Third World than other European countries.

Other traditional aspects of Irish life look the same – but nevertheless are changing. There seem to be as many pubs as ever, but statistics suggest that Irish consumption of alcohol per head is amongst the lowest in Europe. That slur has not halted the 1990s British, American and European love affair with Irish pubs, beer and general entertainment. Throughout the world people consume black pints of stout and enjoy assorted Irish gimcrackery; advertisements for newly devised, 'traditional' Irish beer feature dark Heathcliff-looking youths, smouldering colleens, a horse or two, and assorted priests, hurley players and old women, all of which the ad-men assume (and they must be right) constitute an irresistible appeal. Certainly Irish music has a devoted following, and venerable traditional groups such as the Chieftains have joined forces with ancient rockers like the Belfastman Van Morrison. Traditional Irish dancing has been given a lease of life by the jazzed-up world-wide success of *Riverdance*. Celtic Rock has spawned the Horslips, the Pogues, the Saw Doctors. And then there is one of the world's most famous rock bands over the last fifteen years, U2 … New bands start, and fail, every day; an energetic scene, to put it mildly, brilliantly portrayed by the book and film of Roddy Doyle's *The Commitments*.

Bono in Las Vegas. *The lead singer of U2 – and Ireland's premier rock icon – serenades the desert air in 1997 (right).*

Celtic Rock *has replaced Guinness as Ireland's most potent export, blending the instruments from Irish folk and showbands – accordions, whistles, fiddles – with acoustic guitars, to produce music with international appeal. Andrea Corr (left), who, with her two sisters and brother, make up the Corrs; (below left) Tony Lambert, until he won the Lotto and decided to opt out, a member of the much-loved Saw Doctors; (below right) Shane McGowan of the Pogues.*

Sport in Ireland continues along habitual lines. Soccer has been gaining popularity in the south, flushed by the Republic's successful performances in two recent World Cups. For soccer Ireland's teams are divided north and south, but other sports are represented on an all-Ireland basis – the GAA games, and largely middle-class pursuits such as rugby and golf. Racing continues to exert its pull, as befitting the country which invented steeplechasing. The real business and money is with flat racing, however, and the bloodstock industry plays an important part in the Republic's economy. Many of the famous winners over the last decades have come from Ireland – Red Rum, the Grand National indefatigable, Shergar, who was kidnapped and met a grisly end, and perhaps the most celebrated of them all, Arkle.

Sportsmen. *David O'Leary (right) leaps for joy after scoring the vital final penalty in the shoot-out that decided the Ireland–Romania game in the 1990 World Cup finals. The national side was transformed under the management of Jack Charlton, seen far right with one of his players, Andy Townsend. Neither Big Jack nor Andy is Irish (when he donned Irish green, Townsend became 'the first captain of the Republic to dye for the cause')*

but then neither is the Opel car. (Below right) Pat Taafe on the legendary Arkle outrides fellow Irishman Willie Robinson on Mill House in the 1964 Cheltenham Gold Cup. Barry McGuigan (below), former world featherweight boxing champion, puts on the gloves for another training bout. He became an inspiration to young Ulstermen, catholic and protestant, using the boxing ring as neutral territory where they could meet.

Writers. *(Clockwise from top left) William Trevor (*Fools of Fortune, The Ballroom of Romance)*, twice winner of the Whitbread Prize; Brian Friel the playwright, author of* Translations *and* Dancing at Lughnasa*; Roddy Doyle whose novel* Paddy Clarke Ha Ha Ha *won the Booker Prize in 1995; Maeve Binchy, bestselling novelist; Michael Longley, distinguished poet.* [PHOTOS, CLOCKWISE FROM TOP LEFT: MARK GERSON; BOBBY HANVEY; DONOVAN WYLIE; MARK GERSON; BOBBY HANVEY]

Political parties would appear to have remained unchanged, the two leading ones still Fianna Fail and Fine Gael, but in fact there have been significant developments. There is far less automatic family loyalty to the one or the other. Fiana Fail might be a touch more republican than Fine Gael, as one would expect from its anti-Treaty inception, but again far less than in previous years; on the question of Northern Ireland there has been general cross-party consensus, as indeed in Britain. The Republic's use of proportional representation for its voting has meant the appearance of independents and minority parties, such as the Progressive Democrats, an offshoot of malcontents from Fianna Fail, while Ireland's oldest political party, Labour, has experienced a new lease of life in the 1980s and 1990s, forming government coalitions under its leader Dick Spring. The politician who exerted most fascination on the voters and commentators over the last thirty years undoubtedly has been Charles Haughey, able, ambitious and, in certain areas, unscrupulous.

Throughout the 1980s he duelled with Fine Gael's leader, Garret FitzGerald, a slightly shambolic, intellectual figure. It was said in Dublin that if either found a banknote on the street, Haughey would pocket it, whereas FitzGerald would lose it. Haughey led a charmed political career, seemingly down and disgraced many times, but then surfacing as potent as ever. As another of his political enemies, Conor Cruise O'Brien, remarked in 1982 (after Haughey had been defeated): 'If I saw Mr Haughey buried at midnight at a crossroads, with a stake driven through his heart – politically speaking – I should continue to wear a clove of garlic round my neck, just in case.' Prescient words: for The Boss was to return for another stint in office from 1987 to 1992. But the most impressive politician recently has been the one with the least power – Mary Robinson, President of Ireland from 1990 to 1997. Her election was unexpected, as she was standing against representatives from the two major parties and with only Labour's support; but the Fianna

Power and money. *Prime Minister Charles Haughey, The Boss, in his palmy days (left) when policemen held the door for him instead of investigating his affairs. Irishmen have switched their admiration from him to figures like Michael Smurfit and Tony O'Reilly (right and below), Croesus-like businessmen and performers on the multinational stage with interests spread across a whole range of companies.*

Fail candidate self-destructed and she came through the middle. Previously a vigorous battler for social reform, her tenure as President has been regarded, universally, as an unqualified success, even though her position prevented her from entering the political debates. Her stylish conduct, and careful gestures, gave the country prestige and a badly needed integrity to contrast with the grubby antics of other politicos.

Mary Robinson's comments on Northern Ireland before her election had pleased Unionist leaders, but once in the Presidency she had to operate by symbols. Some of these continued to please Unionists, such as shaking hands with the Queen of England, but others upset them as when she shook hands with the Sinn Fein leader, Gerry Adams, in 1993. Yet what she was demonstrating here was that Sinn Fein could no longer be marginalised after its emergence as a political party in the 1980s with consistent electoral support. Rather than being seen simply as a front for the men of violence, it had to be brought into the political process for any hope of peace in Northern Ireland. It is a lesson which recent governments in Britain too have appeared to learn.

Since the ending of Unionist party rule with the abolition of Stormont in 1972, governments of the Republic have adopted a cross-party approach to the north, and similarly broad agreement with Britain's policies. Such was clearly demonstrated by the first demarche after the imposition of direct rule – the Sunningdale Agreement of 1973, engineered by the British and Irish governments, some (but not all of the Unionists) and the SDLP. This provided for a two-tier Council of Ireland; the first a power-sharing executive in Northern Ireland, led by the Unionist Brian Faulkner with his deputy the nationalist, Gerry Fitt, and remaining ministries shared out between Unionists, SDLP and the Alliance party. The second tier was intended to be a consultative assembly drawn from southern and northern representatives. By agreeing to Sunningdale the southern government accepted the right of Northern Ireland to exist – in contravention to its 1937 constitution – and also that there would be no change to Northern Ireland's status unless the majority decided. Ian Paisley, it should be noted, did not approve; neither, of course, did the IRA which continued its campaign of bombings and killings. Nevertheless the initiative seemed promising; but by jettisoning his previous hard-line position, Faulkner then lost support from a range of unionists. Loyalist groups formed the Ulster Workers Council and arranged a strike aimed at bringing down the executive. Despite firm words from Harold Wilson (who branded the strike a 'deliberate and calculated attempt to use every undemocratic and unparliamentary means ... so as to set up a sectarian and undemocratic state, from which one third of the people would be excluded'), the security forces were not ordered to intervene, Brian Faulkner had to resign – victim of the 'not an inch' philosophy of unionism – and the power-sharing executive collapsed.

So the Troubles continued, claiming 3,270 lives by the

Mary Robinson *(left), President of Ireland from 1990 to 1997, a former barrister, catholic but married to a protestant, is one of the women who broke the male domination of society there. Her background of nationalist and 'British' colonial civil servant relatives made her an even-handed diplomat when it came to Northern Ireland. She brought dignity and influence to the post of President.*
[PHOTO: PETER MARLOW]

Mary McAleese *(below left), the second consecutive woman President of Ireland who succeeded Mary Robinson in 1997. An Ulster catholic academic, and therefore a British citizen, she has to get security clearance when she wishes to return home to Northern Ireland. Still something of an unknown quantity.*
[PHOTO: BOBBY HANVEY]

Monica McWilliams *(right), founder of the Woman's Coalition, on the right in the picture talking to a Party worker. In Northern Ireland she appealed to those who were tired of waiting for the menfolk to see reason, and to the mothers of the dead on both sides.*

Dana *(below right). Derry-born Rosemary Brown, Eurovision Song Contest winner in 1970 and Presidential candidate in 1997. Some were surprised by the good third placing of this one-time American T. V. evangelist, but by 1997 women mattered in Ireland and people admired Dana's honest views. Perhaps the country remembered the pretty young woman who gently sang 'All Kinds of Everything', dressed in the plainest of clothes, save a small Celtic motif. Her home city had been cloaked in violence for over a year and for all the world to see.*

beginning of 1998. The worst year had been 1972, with 470 dead, but since the mid 1970s the yearly toll usually has been 50 to 100. To many in Britain and around the world the struggle has appeared to be between the IRA and the British Army, but after the 1970s the brunt of attacks against the security forces has been borne by the RUC and what was the UDR (now the Royal Irish Regiment), a territorial unit. And the terrorists have not just been the IRA. There have also been a vast number of civilian deaths, many of them sectarian murders by loyalist paramilitaries. Perhaps the most notorious of these were the victims tortured and carved up by the 'Shankill Butchers' who killed a number of catholics *qua* catholics in the 1970s, finally being convicted and imprisoned for 19 murders. It has been estimated that of the almost 1,000 people killed by loyalists in the Troubles, more than 600 have been uninvolved catholics; the rest republican activists. Foreign meddling, largely on the side of the republicans, has stirred the pot: for instance, Irish-Americans through 'Noraid' have been responsible for supplying stronger medicine than just humanitarian relief for the assistance of northern catholics. More openly, Colonel Gaddafi has boasted of running arms to the IRA; at least two shipments from Libya were captured in the 1970s and 1980s, making it likely that others got through. Further sinister influences were revealed by an English reporter in the

The victory of unreason. *A Loyalist bonfire to celebrate the collapse of the 1973 Sunningdale Agreement (right). This had established a power-sharing executive between some Unionist and some Nationalist parties, and the principle of a cross-border, consultative assembly. The extremist Unionists strangled it at birth with a strike, doing the IRA's work for them. Twenty-five years later, with the Good Friday 1998 agreement, we were back to much the same solution – this time, however, with the acquiescence of most gunmen and, one hoped, more resolute British determination to make it work.*

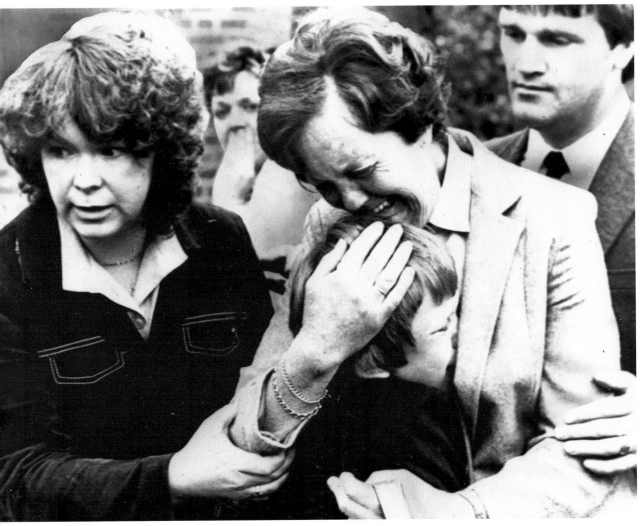

A mother's grief *in 1981 (left). Whose and of what faith no longer signifies in the perspective of history. Her son might not have died if Sunningdale had been given a chance.*

early 1970s, when he achieved a scoop photographing Far Eastern revolutionaries training the Provos. (After the session was over, and the visitor departed, the Chinese waiters were helped out of their paramilitary accoutrements, and allowed back to their restaurant in Derry.)

Over the years there has been a proliferation of acronyms as fresh nationalist and loyalist paramilitaries have emerged. The IRA has split into Provisionals and Officials (the latter dropping out of the struggle after 1972), the Irish National Liberation Army and more recently the shadowy Army Continuity Movement; their counterparts amongst loyalist paramilitaries have included the Ulster Defence Association, Ulster Freedom Fighters, Ulster Volunteer Force, and more recently the Loyalist Volunteer Force. Ethnic cleansing has ensured that the division between the two confessions remains absolute: one official report estimates 60,000 people being forced to leave their homes in 1969–72, some 80 per cent of them catholics driven out by loyalists. Until Yugoslavia fell apart in the 1990s, this was the largest forced movement of a population within Europe since the Second World War. In

Miltown Cemetery *and the grenade lobbed by a Loyalist, Michael Stone, into the crowd of spectators at a big IRA funeral in March 1988 has just gone off, making them cower behind the gravestones. They were there to see the burial of members of the IRA bomb squad shot in Gibraltar by an SAS team before they could carry out their mission. On 14 May 1998, Stone was given a rapturous welcome at Belfast City Hall by a gathering of hardline Loyalists. Stone was a freelance killer working for no one. He was considered too extreme and too unpredictable for even the UVF and the UDA; they both saw him as a 'liability'.*
[PHOTO: CHRIS STEELE-PERKINS]

general terms republican tactics have had one simple aim: 'the way to get rid of you British', an IRA man explained to a government representative in 1972, 'as has been proved all over your Empire, is violence. You will get fed-up and go away.' The British response for many years was equally forth-right: the IRA were terrorists who had to be defeated militarily in order to bring peace to Northern Ireland. It might be said that the republicans misread Northern Ireland as just another colonial trouble-spot for the British, by conveniently ignoring the protestant majority; and that the British failed to act suc-cessfully on Mao's famous advice that, to defeat the terrorist, his sympathetic population had to be converted, which in northern terms meant some constitutional initiative.

The first of these attempts after the Sunningdale debacle, was the Anglo-Irish Agreement signed by Margaret Thatcher and Garret FitzGerald in 1985. In part this was a response to the meteoric rise of Sinn Fein, itself the consequence of the government's defeat of the hunger strike at the Maze prison where ten men, including Bobby Sands, briefly an MP, starved themselves to death in 1981, attempting to regain the special conditions akin to PoW status originally allowed to imprisoned terrorists. The Agreement allowed the Dublin government a

Agitprop. *School children (above) being indoctrinated by a reinactment of IRA prisoners' 'dirty protests' of the late 1970s, when they only wore blankets and smeared their own excrement on their cell walls.* [PHOTO: KLAUS FRANCKE]

Last rites *by Fr. Alec Reid said over the body of one of the two British Army corporals (right) killed at Andersonstown when, losing their way, they encountered an IRA funeral procession three days after the Miltown Cemetery incident in March 1988. One of them pulled a pistol and fired into the air, then the mob engulfed them, even though there was an Army helicopter hover-ing overhead. Taken away by car, tortured, beaten and stripped, their bodies were then dumped. Even in the catalogue of Northern Ireland's killings, these were particularly brutal deaths.*

say in Northern Ireland affairs through the establishment of the Anglo-Irish Conference – which continues to meet today. Once again the Irish government recognised the status of Northern Ireland and that no change could come without consent of the majority; but that did not stop the howl of protest from unionists. Mrs Thatcher, however, was not going to allow Loyalist mobs to smash any of *her* decisions, and she instructed the security forces to hold firm. In the short term, the Agreement did succeed in marginalising Sinn Fein: its overall vote fell by 2 per cent in the 1987 General Election, and Adams lost his Belfast seat. But Sinn Fein regained its level of support in the early 1990s and the old stalemate reappeared. Meanwhile the violence continued; in the month of October 1993 alone, twenty-seven people in the north were killed, most by Loyalist gunmen.

John Hume, amongst others, has been credited with brokering the eventual ceasefire entered into by the IRA in August 1994. He had been in on-off negotiations with Gerry Adams since 1988 and, despite ritual disclaimers from Adams that he could not speak for the Provisionals, it was clear that they might well follow what Sinn Fein decided. In the early 1990s the British government was also engaged in secret talks with the IRA (strenuously denied at the time, later admitted) and there began to arise the hope that Sinn Fein and the IRA might give up the armed campaign in return for some kind of self-determination on the future of Northern Ireland, plus Sinn Fein's entry into talks for a resolution. The Irish Prime Minister, Albert Reynolds, and the British Prime Minister, John Major, after some tough meetings, issued the Downing Street Declaration in December 1993. Although this mentioned the possibility of a united Ireland, it did confirm the need for majority consent in Northern Ireland – in essence the old unionist veto. Ian Paisley managed to interpret it as Major selling 'Ulster to buy off the fiendish Republican scum'; but Sinn Fein were perhaps more realistic in sounding dissent. Nevertheless, the mood was changing, the laws censoring Sinn Fein representatives were lifted, and in August 1994 the IRA announced a ceasefire; six weeks later loyalist paramilitaries followed suit.

Very soon, however, the British government was complaining that the ceasefire was not 'permanent'; then, when some months had passed and the ceasefire held, that the IRA should surrender their arms. Until that time no talks with Sinn Fein could begin. This was the issue which led to the end of the first ceasefire seventeen months later. Although a huge IRA bomb at Canary Wharf in London dramatically signalled this change, the violence never really recommenced in Northern Ireland. And in fact in July 1997 the IRA renewed its ceasefire, while Sinn Fein was promised admission to all-party talks. Various paramilitary factions did not subscribe to this second ceasefire – INLA for the republicans, the LVF for the unionists – but amidst suspicions and temporary expulsions, representatives for the other groups started meeting at last in 1998.

Finally on Friday 10 April 1998 an agreement based on Senator Mitchell's proposals was reached between the British

Ingredients for peace? *Gerry Adams (far right) and Martin McGuinness (near right), the Sinn Fein leaders, with David Trimble, the head of the Ulster Unionists (below them, right) have come some way from their positions in the 1970s. Trimble was one of the wreckers of the Sunningdale Agreement, while McGuinness and Adams were close to, if not in, the IRA front line. The peacebrokers who got them to the table are on the left: John Hume of the SDLP (top) and the retired US Senator George Mitchell (below).*
[PHOTO, TOP LEFT: BOBBY HANVEY]

and Irish governments and, not least, between the major Unionist party, the SDLP and Sinn Fein. This provided for a Northern Ireland Assembly with an eventual power-sharing executive, plus certain north–south links across the border. In the next few weeks David Trimble managed to sell the settlement to his Unionist party, and Gerry Adams the same to Sinn Fein. Vociferous elements from both unionist and nationalist communities condemned the deal as a sell-out (for their respective faiths) but the two referendums on 22 May produced a clear majority in favour: 71 per cent from the North and 94 per cent from the South.

As Ireland moves towards the 21st century, the fury of the

Seamus Heaney *on Dublin's North Wall. From northern catholic stock, but with a readership for his poetry all over the English-speaking world, he can stand for the transcendence of tribal hatred and the continuing gifts of literature which Ireland offers up.*
[PHOTO: BOBBY HANVEY]

past thirty years appears to be ending. Of course, once uttered, such a hope looks foolish, almost guaranteed to herald a fresh round of violence and killing. Past commentators have had such predictions shattered. But the big picture seems to have changed in the last few years. On one level the unionists have won: over the key question of land and sovereignty, Northern Ireland remains British and will continue to be British as long as the majority in that place wish it so. Most Irish nationalists accept this conclusion; southern governments have been doing so for over twenty years – in 1993, 1985 and 1973. (This is one reason why removing Articles 2 and 3 of the Republic's constitution – much agitated for by some – will change noth-ing, not least entrenched unionist attitudes in the north; it will, however, remove the excuse for their actions that these Articles present.) The men of violence, those heirs to the physical force men of the 19th and 20th centuries, have lost: a united Ireland established by force of arms will never happen. Yet at another level, the nationalists have won. The old Northern Ireland, with its sectarian one-party rule is dead and buried; cross-border links with the Republic of Ireland, unthinkable thirty years ago, have been operating since 1985 and look set to continue in one form or another; the minority in the north is flourishing and confident. 'Is there life before death?' ran one mordant graffito seen in Belfast in the grim 1970s. At last the answer might be Yes.

BIBLIOGRAPHY

Of the vast quantity of books on 20th-century Ireland, the following have been most useful for this essay. For general political history, F. S. L. Lyons, *Ireland Since the Famine* (1973); J. J. Lee, *Ireland, 1912–1985* (1989); R. F. Foster, *Modern Ireland, 1600–1972* (1988). R. F. Foster, *Paddy and Mr Punch* (1993), offers further insight into cultural matters. To understand the Anglo-Irish world, Elizabeth Bowen, *Bowen's Court* (1942), is essential, as is Mark Bence-Jones, *Twilight of the Ascendancy* (1987), packed with revealing anecdotes, and mined shamelessly for this piece. Aspects of the Irish literary revival at the turn of the century and its effects on Irish identity are examined in the early chapters of Conor Cruise O'Brien, *States of Ireland* (1974). George Moore's autobiography of this period, *Hail and Farewell* (1914), is sly, sardonic and amusing. For Ulster's resistance to Home Rule see A. T. Q. Stewart, *The Ulster Crisis* (1967). George Dangerfield, *The Strange Death of Liberal England* (1935), which covers the crisis, is dated, unreliable and unfair to the unionists – but enormous fun to read. He becomes more restrained and reliable with *The Damnable Question* (1977) which looks at the 1916 Rising. The Anglo-Irish war is best covered by Charles Townshend, *The British Campaign in Ireland, 1919–21* (1975), and the same author's *Political Violence in Ireland* (1983). Carlton Younger, *Ireland's Civil War* (1968), examines a still murky episode. Of the many biographies on Michael Collins, those by Rex Taylor (1958) and T. P. Coogan (1990) have been most helpful. Independent Ireland in the social and cultural desert before the 1960s can be seen from a foreigner's perspective in Heinrich Boll, *Irish Journal* (1957); an American's perspective in the excellent sketch by Donal Connery, *The Irish* (1968); and the eyes of the essayist Hubert Butler, *Escape from the Anthill* (1985). Literary gossip is provided by John Ryan, *Remembering How We Stood* (1987). Political developments are dealt with in Ronan Fanning, *Independent Ireland* (1983). The definitive book on Ireland during the Second World War is Robert Fisk, *In Time of War* (1985); further stories come from Tony Gray, *The Lost Years* (1997). Northern Ireland is covered judiciously by David Harkness, *Northern Ireland Since 1920* (1983), and more passionately by T. P. Coogan, *The Troubles* (1996). Two older works on the North remain essential: Conor Cruise O'Brien's book (above) and Dervla Murphy, *A Place Apart* (1978). For the men of violence, Patrick Bishop and Eamonn Mallie, *The Provisional IRA* (1987) and Peter Taylor, *Provos: The IRA and Sinn Fein* (1997), seem as accurate as possible. Down south, John Ardagh, *Ireland and the Irish* (1994), captures the new modern state. Finally, a bouquet to that admirable journal *History Ireland*, running since 1993 and full of interesting re-assessments and out of the way information.

(Left) 'The Raider', a photograph by Fr. Browne S. J., Dublin 1948.

ACKNOWLEDGEMENTS

We would like to thank especially the following people for their kind help, advice and expertise:

Ken Anderson, Ulster Folk & Transport Museum; Rachel Bowtel and Leni McCullagh, Radio Telefis Eireann and The Cashman Collection; Nick Coveney; David and Edwin Davison, Davison & Associates Ltd and The Fr. F. M. Browne S. J. Collection/Irish Picture Library; Mrs G. A. Duncan; Patrick and Lady Anthea Forde; Klaus Francke; Tom Graves, Weidenfeld & Nicolson; Desmond Fitzgerald, The Knight of Glin; Bobby Hanvey; David and Judy Lindsay; Grainne Machlouchlain, National Library of Ireland; Pat McLean, Ulster Museum; Nick Nugent; Derek Speirs.

Picture acknowledgements

Allsport UK Ltd, London: 217TL, 217TR
Connaught Tribune, Galway, Republic of Ireland: 210
Davison & Associates Ltd & The Fr. Browne S. J. Collection/Irish Picture Library, Dublin, Republic of Ireland: 5, 13, 41, 57, 61, 74TL, 75, 88, 89, 116, 129, 133, 142T, 143, 144, 152, 175, 176, 178, 234, 237.
Mrs G. A. Duncan, Dublin, Republic of Ireland: 4, 149, 150T, 150B, 151, 154, 156, 168, 174.
Bobby Hanvey, Downpatrick, Northern Ireland: 161, 191, 198, 202, 206B, 218BL, 219L, 222B, 230T, 232–233.
Arthur J. England Collection, Dublin, Republic of Ireland: 66L.
Tom Graves: 36, 155.
Mark Gerson, London: 218TL, 219BR.
Klaus Francke, Hamburg, Germany: 166–67 (all photos), 190, 206, 207, 211, 228.
Hulton Getty Picture Collection, London: 1, 6, 9, 12, 24, 30, 37M, 37R, 38, 39, 44, 45T, 45B, 46, 52, 53T, 53B, 54T, 54BL, 54BR, 56, 58, 60T, 60B, 62, 64, 65, 68–69 (all photos), 71, 72, 73, 76, 77, 78, 79, 80T, 80B, 81, 82, 83, 84, 87, 92, 93, 94, 95, 96, 97, 98, 99, 100, 101, 102, 104, 106, 107L, 107R, 108, 109, 110, 111, 112, 114T, 114B, 117, 118, 119, 120, 121, 123T, 123B, 125, 126, 127, 132, 134T, 134B, 135, 136, 142B, 146, 147, 148, 153L, 153R, 162L, 162R, 163L, 163R, 164L, 164R, 165L, 165R, 169T, 169B, 171, 172, 173, 177, 183, 184, 186, 187, 188, 189, 192, 193L, 193R, 194, 195T, 195B, 196, 199, 200, 201, 203, 216, 217B, 224, 225.
Imperial War Museum, London: 67, 74B.
Irish Times, Dublin, Republic of Ireland: 170T, 170B.
Lensmen, Dublin, Republic of Ireland: 140, 179, 180, 181, 213R, 220.
Magnum Photos, London: 197, 219TR, 222T, 226–27.
National Library of Ireland, Dublin, Republic of Ireland: 22, 31, 59, 115, 122, 160, 182.
National Museum of Ireland, Dublin, Republic of Ireland: 42.
Pacemaker, Belfast, Northern Ireland: 223T, 230B, 231T, 231B.
Redferns, London: 212, 213L, 214–15 (all photos), 223B.
Rex Features, London: 221T, 221B.
R. T. E. & The Cashman Collection, Dublin, Republic of Ireland: 63, 85, 91, 103, 130, 131, 138, 138T, 139B, 145, 158–59 (all photos).
Sean Sexton/Hulton Getty Collection, London: 10, 17R, 20T, 20–21 (all photos), 23, 29, 43.
Slide File, Dublin, Republic of Ireland: 205.
Derek Speirs/Report, Dublin, Republic of Ireland: 208
Ulster Museum, Belfast, Northern Ireland: 15, 17L, 19, 26, 35, 40.
Ulster Folk & Transport Museum, Belfast, Northern Ireland: 2–3, 18T, 18B, 25, 27, 32, 33, 34, 48, 50, 51.
Weidenfeld Archive, Weidenfeld & Nicolson, London: 37L.

Whilst every effort has been made to trace and acknowledge all copyright holders, we would like to apologize should there be any errors or omissions.

The following poems have been reproduced with the permission of the publishers or literary agents. In the United Kingdom: p.43, 'A Coat'; p.85, extract from 'Sixteen Dead Men', both taken from *The Collected Poems of W. B. Yeats*, reproduced by kind permission of A. P. Watt Ltd on behalf of Michael Yeats. In the U.S.A.: reprinted with the permission of Scribner, a Division of Simon & Schuster, from THE COLLECTED WORKS OF W.B. YEATS, Volume 1: THE POEMS, revised and edited by Richard J. Finneran. Copyright © 1916, 1924 by Macmillan Publishing Company; copyright renewed 1944, 1952 by Bertha Georgie Yeats. On p.191, the extract from Seamus Heaney's *North* is published with the permission of Faber and Faber (U.K.) and of Farrar, Straus & Giroux (U.S.A.).

Author's note: I should like to thank Charles Merullo, whose conception this was; Richard Collins, whose calmness ensured the project came in on schedule; Bill Bagnell, for providing not just the pictures but nuggets of information on things Irish; and not least Roger Hudson for editorial skills and captions, and invaluable suggestions and advice.

(Right) Fusiliers Arch, St Stephen's Green, Dublin, 1945. Built to commemorate the men of the Royal Dublin Fusiliers killed in the Boer War. A photograph by Fr. Browne S. J.

INDEX

Page numbers in *italics* refer
to captions to illustrations